Climate Change:
OUR WARMING EARTH

Essential Library

An Imprint of Abdo Publishing | www.abdopublishing.com

History of
Science

Climate Change:
OUR WARMING EARTH

by Carol Hand

Content Consultant
Dr. Spencer Weart
American Institute of Physics

History of Science

www.abdopublishing.com

Published by Abdo Publishing, a division of ABDO, PO Box 398166, Minneapolis, Minnesota 55439. Copyright © 2015 by Abdo Consulting Group, Inc. International copyrights reserved in all countries. No part of this book may be reproduced in any form without written permission from the publisher. Essential Library™ is a trademark and logo of Abdo Publishing.

Printed in the United States of America, North Mankato, Minnesota

102014
012015

Cover Photos: Photobank Gallery/Shutterstock Images; Michael Warwick/Shutterstock Images; Image Post/Shutterstock Images
Interior Photos: Photobank Gallery/Shutterstock Images, 1, 3; Michael Warwick/Shutterstock Images, 1, 3; Image Post/Shutterstock Images, 1, 3; Extreme Ice Survey/AP Images, 7; Nabil K. Mark/Centre Daily Times/AP Images, 9; Roger Ressmeyer/Corbis, 10, 71; James Balog/GDA/AP Images, 13; NASA, 15, 49; North Wind Picture Archives, 17; dieKleinert/SuperStock, 19; Hulton-Deutsch Collection/Corbis, 21, 29; Mondadori/Getty Images, 24; Arthur Green/Bettmann/Corbis, 27; Mark Garlick/Science Source, 31; Bettmann/Corbis, 35; AP Images, 37, 39; Chris Stewart/AP Images, 41; Jim Sugar/Corbis, 42; NOAA, 44, 57, 80; iStockphoto, 47; Morton Beebe/Corbis, 51; Peter Zaharov/Shutterstock Images, 53; Bernhard Staehli/Shutterstock Images, 59; Gareth Fuller/PA Wire/AP Images, 60; NASA/Goddard Institute for Space Studies/Science Source, 62; Ian Barrett/CP/AP Images, 66; Alan Marler/AP Images, 69; Chiaki Tsukumo/AP Images, 73; Julia Moore/Medford Mail Tribune/AP Images, 76; Tony Gutierrez/AP Images, 79; US National Snow and Ice Data Center/AP Images, 81; Bullit Marquez/AP Images, 84; NickolayLamm/Splash News/Corbis, 87; Phil Klein/AP Images, 89; Rex Features/AP Images, 93; Department of Energy, 96

Editor: Arnold Ringstad
Series Designer: Craig Hinton

Library of Congress Control Number: 2014943865

Cataloging-in-Publication Data
Hand, Carol.
 Climate change: our warming Earth / Carol hand.
  p. cm. -- (History of science)
ISBN 978-1-62403-558-6 (lib. bdg.)
Includes bibliographical references and index.
1. Climatology--History--Juvenile literature. 2. Weather--Juvenile literature. 3. Global warming--Juvenile literature. 4. Climate--Juvenile literature. I. Title.
551.6--dc23

                                             2014943865

Contents

The Hockey Stick
OF CLIMATE

$$\frac{a+b}{a} = \frac{a}{b} = 1{,}618$$

Average global temperatures on Earth rose 1.53 degrees Fahrenheit (0.85°C) between 1880 and 2012.[1] More than half of this warming has occurred since 1979. Higher temperatures are causing rapid melting of Arctic and Antarctic ice and mountain glaciers, decreases in overall snow cover, warmer oceans, and rising sea levels. They are also making extreme weather events more frequent. These stronger storms, worse droughts and floods, and heavier snowfalls lead to human deaths and destruction of property. People are seeing the results of global warming on Earth and in their own lives. Many species may go extinct as a result of climate change.

At least 97 percent of climate scientists now agree this warming most likely results from human activities.[2] A key cause is the burning of fossil fuels. When fossil fuels are burned, they release gases into the atmosphere, including carbon dioxide. This

Cameras designed to monitor
Arctic glaciers have recorded direct
evidence of increased melting.

and other gases help the atmosphere retain more heat from the sun, warming the planet. This concept reached broad acceptance in the scientific community relatively recently. Throughout the 1900s, scientists wondered whether increased levels of carbon dioxide and other gases could actually raise global temperatures. They debated whether humans could really change the climate, and if so, how significantly.

What Is the Hockey Stick Graph?

In 1998, Michael Mann of the University of Massachusetts decided to follow the evidence. Along with Raymond S. Bradley, also of the University of Massachusetts, and Malcolm K. Hughes of the University of Arizona, he analyzed data for ancient climates in the Northern Hemisphere. The scientists used data from fossil tree rings, ice cores, and ancient corals. These objects can be studied, measured, and analyzed to determine the approximate temperatures during the time they formed. They combined this ancient data with modern thermometer readings collected since the mid-1800s. The result was a continuous reconstruction of Northern Hemisphere temperatures going back 1,000 years. Mann and his colleagues published their report in the scientific journal *Geophysical Research Letters*.

One key part of the report was a graph showing average Northern Hemisphere temperatures over the last millennium. It soon became known as the hockey stick graph. Temperatures were relatively flat for the first 900 years. This made up the long handle of the hockey stick. In the last century, and especially in the last several

Mann has become a major public face for the issues surrounding climate change.

decades, the graph spiked sharply upward, creating the stick's blade. The graph was featured in the 2001 report of the Intergovernmental Panel on Climate Change (IPCC), a scientific body set up by the members of the United Nations. It became an iconic illustration of human influence on climate. Mann summarized its significance: "The graph told a simple story: that a sharp and highly unusual rise in atmospheric

Data from ice cores can be used to infer temperatures from the distant past.

warming was occurring on Earth. Furthermore, that rise seemed to coincide with human-caused increases in greenhouse gas levels due to the burning of fossil fuels."[3]

Proxy Data: What and Why?

To understand how the climate operates, scientists must understand that changing climates have existed throughout Earth's history. But, while Earth is 4.54 billion years old, humans have been directly collecting weather data for less than 200 years.[4]

The only way scientists can understand older climates is to study objects that remain from ancient times and that have recorded some aspect of the climate. These natural recorders provide proxy data. In general, a proxy is an indirect measurement that serves as a substitute or representative. Here, the proxy data stands in for thermometer data.

Mann's graph was based on proxy data from the past 1,000 years, combined with actual temperature measurements when available. Much of the proxy data consisted of tree ring data from various locations and ice cores from Greenland and Peru. Mann's first graph, created in 1998, went back 600 years and included more than 100 data sets. A revised version made in 1999 extended back a full millennium. However, only 12 tree ring and two ice core data sets were available for the years before 1400.[5]

Piecing together information on ancient climates is difficult. Some data sets are sparse, and data becomes less available the farther back in time one goes. The authors carefully described the graph's limitations and uncertainties. They also validated the proxy data by comparing proxy data with direct thermometer data wherever possible.

WHAT PROXY DATA TELLS US

Each type of proxy data leads to temperature estimates in a different way.

+ Annual tree rings vary in width and density according to temperature and precipitation. Trees may live for hundreds or thousands of years.

+ Ocean and lake sediments build up in layers; the deepest layers are the oldest. Sediment cores are analyzed for pollen grains, shells, and chemicals.

+ Coral skeletons are composed of calcium carbonate. Oxygen isotopes in the calcium carbonate vary depending on the water temperature in which the coral grew.

+ Ice cores from the Greenland and Antarctic ice sheets date back hundreds of thousands of years. The temperature estimates are determined by studying pockets of air trapped within the cores and analyzing the oxygen isotopes in each layer.

For example, they compared temperature data collected using thermometers between 1854 and 1901 with proxy data from tree rings for the same time period. The two data sets matched, indicating that the proxy data was valid.

The Hockey Stick after 15 Years

Other scientists did not automatically accept the hockey stick graph. As with all scientific claims, the conclusions of Mann and his colleagues would have to be independently tested and reproduced. This would provide strong evidence for the graph's validity. Since the 1999 publication, scientists and organizations have assessed Mann's data and done their own temperature reconstructions. They used different statistical techniques and different proxy data. The reconstructions all showed the 1900s contained the strongest warming trend in the past 500 years.[6]

In 2003, Mann and British climate scientist Philip Jones published an updated analysis with additional data, extending the reconstruction back 2,000 years. By 2004, a dozen reconstructions and new models had been done. All of them validated Mann's original hockey stick graph. Some showed greater variability than the original graph, but all showed

Who Is Michael Mann?

Michael E. Mann is now a Distinguished Professor of Meteorology at Pennsylvania State University and director of the university's Earth System Science Center. Mann received his bachelor's degree in physics and applied math from the University of California at Berkeley. He went on to receive a master's degree in physics and a doctorate in geology and geophysics from Yale University. Mann was a lead author on a chapter in a 2001 report produced by the IPCC. He has received many awards and honors for his work in understanding Earth's climate.

Researchers travel to the Arctic to document the effects of climate change.

the rapid and unusual upsurge in temperature during the late 1900s. A 2006 report by the US National Academy of Sciences vouched for its validity.

In 2013, a new study published in the journal *Science* used data from 73 sites around the world to reconstruct Earth's climate back to the end of the last ice age, more than 10,000 years ago.[7] Scientists determined today's temperatures are warmer than they have been for the past 9,040 years.[8] These results are significant because they are global and because they span the entire history of human civilization. Also, they show the climate slowly cooled by approximately 1.3 degrees Fahrenheit (0.72°C) over the last 5,000 years—until 100 years ago. Since then, it has warmed the same amount in only 100 years.[9] This extremely rapid rate of warming worries scientists.

RISING TEMPERATURES

This graph shows how global temperatures compare to a baseline average from the period 1951–1980. The black boxes represent the average temperature from each year. The red line follows the running five-year average temperature. The graph shows a large increase in temperature since 1979.

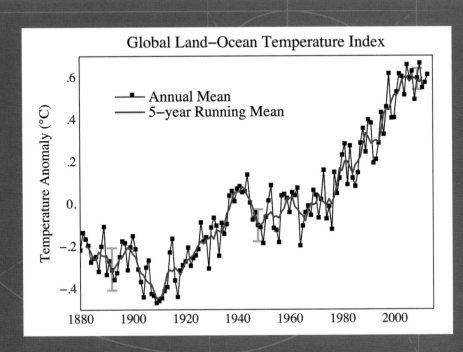

Writers, politicians, and a few scientists have attacked the validity of the hockey stick graph. They have criticized the data, the statistical methods, and even the honesty and motivations of its authors. Climate scientists have successfully answered each criticism. They have explained misunderstandings and pointed out opposing claims based on false assumptions. The scientific consensus surrounding the issue has cemented the hockey stick graph as an icon illustrating human-caused climate change.

The modern understanding of climate change is the result of more than a century of work by dedicated scientists. They include physicists, chemists, geologists, and climatologists. The evidence these scientists collected and interpreted has established climate science as a major field of study. It has become especially important in the early 2000s because of its potentially serious consequences for the planet.

THE HOCKEY STICK AND THE CLIMATE CRITICS

In the United States, many people criticize the science of climate change. They do not believe climate change is occurring. Many are politicians and members of industries that might sustain economic damage if the United States took steps to fight climate change. For instance, the fossil fuel industry might be hurt if people bought and burned less oil, coal, and natural gas. Many have gone to great lengths to discredit the hockey stick graph. Although climate scientists have successfully rebutted many scientific critiques, politically motivated attacks persist. Retired physicist S. Fred Singer calls the hockey stick graph a "manufactured item" that "does not correspond to well-established historic reality."[10] Senator James Inhofe of Oklahoma declared global warming a "hoax."[11]

Chapter Two

The Early Years
OF CLIMATE SCIENCE

$$\frac{a + b}{a} = \frac{a}{b} = 1{,}618$$

Although they were unaware of it, the nations and industries propelling the Industrial Revolution were paving the way for rapid climate change. Throughout the 1800s, rural farm-based societies in Europe and North America gave way to urban societies. New machines made work easier. Mass production in large factories replaced small-scale home manufacturing. Iron and coal mining provided raw materials and power to run factories. The steam engine and railroads made transportation faster and more efficient. Land was cleared, sanitation improved, and populations soared. A second Industrial Revolution, between 1870 and 1910, introduced chemicals, widespread electricity, and major public health advances. Population and industrial growth rates increased further. These advances caused severe air pollution, including black smoke from burning coal. Carbon dioxide and

The extraction of coal from the ground gave the Industrial Revolution a key power source.

other gases, locked up in coal deposits for millions of years, were released into the atmosphere. Human activity began slowly influencing the climate.

In the early 1900s, true climate science did not exist. Science began answering questions about weather, but the broader picture of climate over a long period of time was unknown. Farmers wanted to know when to plant and harvest crops, how much rain they could expect, and when it would occur. Engineers needed to determine when and where they could build dams, bridges, and other structures for the new technological civilization. To solve these problems, people collected regional data on temperature and rainfall. Weather changed with the seasons, but people believed they could count on climate to stay the same. New England winters were cold and snowy. Farther south, they were more moderate. To most people, climate was an unchanging fact of nature.

Discovering Greenhouse Gases

As long ago as the early 1800s, a few scientists were curious about how climate worked. Several made discoveries that eventually became the basis for modern climate science. They discovered that some gases in the atmosphere can trap heat. This trapped heat results in a greenhouse effect that warms the planet.

The French physicist Jean-Baptiste Joseph Fourier discovered the greenhouse effect in 1824. Fourier hypothesized that certain atmospheric gases could trap heat from the sun. He knew Earth was heated by the sun. He hypothesized that some of

Greenhouse gases, *green*, trap solar energy, *yellow*, reflecting some of it, *red*, back to the surface.

WHAT ARE THE GREENHOUSE GASES?

The greenhouse effect results primarily from the "major" greenhouse gases. Most "minor" greenhouse gases are synthetic gases emitted only by human activity. It is difficult to determine exactly how much each gas contributes to the greenhouse effect, because contributions vary depending on conditions.

Major Greenhouse Gases

+ Water vapor (H_2O)
+ Water vapor and cloud droplets (H_2O)
+ Carbon dioxide (CO_2)
+ Methane (CH_4)
+ Ozone (O_3)

Minor Greenhouse Gases

+ Nitrous oxide (N_2O)
+ Sulfur hexafluoride (S_F6)
+ Hydrofluorocarbons (HFCs)
+ Perfluorocarbons (PFCs)
+ Chlorofluorocarbons (CFCs)

this heat bounced off Earth's surface and radiated back into space. The heat gain and loss would need to balance to maintain Earth's steady temperature. Fourier's key insight was the idea that Earth's temperature was directly related to the amount of infrared radiation it received.

Another climate science pioneer was Irish scientist John Tyndall. In 1859, Tyndall conducted a series of experiments testing the ability of various gases to absorb heat. He found that several gases common in the atmosphere, including nitrogen, oxygen, and hydrogen, were nearly transparent. In other words, heat passed through them without being absorbed. However, other gases, including water vapor, carbon dioxide, and ozone, absorbed heat very well. Tyndall concluded these heat-absorbing gases controlled Earth's temperature. He speculated that changes in the amounts of these gases would cause changes in climate.

Carbon Dioxide and Changing Climate

Swedish scientist Svante Arrhenius was the first person to calculate temperature changes resulting from changing

Arrhenius won the Nobel Prize for Chemistry in 1903.

atmospheric carbon dioxide levels. He also studied the physics of Earth, the oceans, and the atmosphere. He wanted to determine if differing levels of heat-absorbing gases could have caused ice ages. In 1896, he calculated that decreasing carbon

How Do Greenhouse Gases Work?

Greenhouse gases absorb infrared radiation, or heat, and transmit it within the atmosphere. This powerful greenhouse effect, which keeps the planet warm, results from a small percentage of atmospheric gases—primarily water vapor, carbon dioxide, methane, and ozone. Each type of greenhouse gas molecule absorbs heat. This causes the molecule to vibrate more rapidly. As vibrating molecules bump into each other, they pass the heat energy back and forth, heating up the atmosphere.

dioxide levels by half would lower Europe's temperature by 7–9 degrees Fahrenheit (4–5°C), enough to start an ice age.[1]

Arrhenius and a colleague, Arvid Högbom, also observed the rate at which human industrial processes were adding carbon dioxide to the atmosphere. Arrhenius calculated that doubling atmospheric dioxide would raise Earth's temperature by 9–11 degrees Fahrenheit (5–6°C).[2] He also calculated that, based on 1896 emission rates, it would take several thousand years for carbon dioxide levels to double. By 1908, when he published more detailed results, industrial levels of carbon dioxide emission had already risen rapidly, and he calculated warming might occur within centuries rather than millennia. However, Arrhenius was more interested in the cause of ice ages than in the potential for future global warming.

By considering only carbon dioxide, Arrhenius greatly oversimplified the climate system. However, he intuitively understood one factor that eluded other scientists of his day. He knew that as air warms, it holds more water vapor. With this in mind, he hypothesized that as increasing carbon dioxide caused air temperature to increase, the amount of water vapor would also increase. Increased water vapor would amplify heating effects. Arrhenius incorporated the effect of water vapor into his calculations. He also understood that carbon dioxide remains in the atmosphere for centuries, while water vapor, which is highly sensitive to temperature changes, cycles in and out of the atmosphere within days. Thus, levels of carbon dioxide would strongly affect levels of water vapor and therefore atmospheric temperature. Although Arrhenius was correct, it would be a century before scientists verified and accepted his hypothesis.

The First Global Carbon Model

Another scientist who studied the effects of carbon dioxide in the late 1800s and early 1900s was American geologist T. C. Chamberlin. Like Arrhenius, Chamberlin was more interested in past ice ages than in the future possibility of global warming. He also understood that carbon dioxide regulated atmospheric temperature, and he wondered how it was stored and transferred through the environment and organisms. Chamberlin's major contribution was the recognition that carbon dioxide levels and climate are not static but instead involve many interacting global processes. He built on Arrhenius's work, explaining his hypothesis as follows: carbon dioxide regulates the daily changes in the amount of water vapor and controls the long-term cycles that cause ice ages. Carbon dioxide enters the atmosphere through volcanic activity and leaves when it combines with minerals in rocks and soil. Lower volcanic activity decreases atmospheric carbon dioxide. If the decrease continues, the

Chamberlin, a prominent geologist, founded the *Journal of Geology*, which is still in print today.

cooling effect spirals the planet into an ice age. Cooling causes the oceans to absorb more carbon dioxide, further lowering the gas's atmospheric concentration. Reversing this entire process causes a warming cycle.

Using the limited data available, in 1897 Chamberlin made rough calculations for the movement of carbon— that is, he built the first primitive carbon model. The results suggested atmospheric carbon dioxide cycled through the system every few thousand years. Chamberlin speculated that changes in the levels of carbon dioxide might at some point make conditions unsuitable for life. Other scientists of the time were unconvinced. They thought carbon dioxide changes occurred on a much longer time scale. They contended that, from the human viewpoint, climate was stable and unchanging. They dismissed Chamberlin's ideas as they had dismissed those of Arrhenius. It was several decades before their contributions were rediscovered. Although these early calculations were crude, later scientists realized the basic ideas were essentially correct. Carbon dioxide, despite its very small concentration in the atmosphere, was primarily responsible for controlling global temperatures.

KEEPING ENERGY IN THE ATMOSPHERE

Some scientists objected to the work of Arrhenius and Chamberlin because they thought there was so much carbon dioxide in the atmosphere that heat absorption was already at a maximum. They based this assumption on experiments later found to be inaccurate. Also, few scientists recognized the existence of atmospheric layers and their effect on energy content. One who did was Nils Ekholm. In 1901, Ekholm explained that energy radiated from Earth's surface moves slowly upward through several atmospheric layers and eventually escapes from the highest layer. The thicker the layers, the more heat can be absorbed in the atmosphere. Also, the higher the last layer is, the colder it will be relative to ground temperature. Thus, compared to lower layers, it will be able to absorb relatively more heat, releasing less into space.

Chapter Three

Climate Science
IN THE EARLY 1900s

$$\frac{a+b}{a} = \frac{a}{b} = 1.618$$

Between 1910 and 1950, industrialization in the United States and Europe continued to increase. Two world wars devastated parts of the world with terrible weapons, including the atomic bomb. Industrialization led to the rise of the oil industry. By the end of World War II (1939–1945), 75 percent of the world's economy resided in the industrialized regions of Europe, North America, the Union of Soviet Socialist Republics (USSR), and Japan.[1] The Cold War, an ideological standoff between the communist USSR and the democratic United States, pitted the two nations against each other in a struggle that never involved direct combat.

Meanwhile, industrialization and advances in technology profoundly changed the global environment. Artificial fertilizers revolutionized agriculture, and food production increased. Advances in medicine and sanitation lowered death rates

Planned suburbs increased the land area of US cities in the mid-1900s.

while birth rates remained high, leading to explosive population growth. People in industrialized countries flocked to urban areas. Cities and agriculture rapidly swallowed up natural areas. Forests were cut down and soil erosion stripped the land of nutrients. People consumed more energy and resources and produced more waste. Coal and oil production boomed, spewing pollution into the atmosphere. Millions of people died of air pollution–related diseases.[2] The fossil fuel era had gone into high gear, and climate change accelerated.

Tracking an Unchanging Climate

Early professional climate scientists, known as climatologists, were unaware rapid industrialization was causing climate changes. Their job was to collect and tabulate data on daily weather. The data could then be used to observe broader climate trends. These detailed weather records would later become a gold mine for climate scientists seeking to understand climate change. But at the time, climate was still considered unchanging. By the mid-1900s, even those who practiced it described climatology as "the dullest branch of meteorology."[3]

Because climatologists had almost no knowledge of the complex processes behind weather, they made no calculations or predictions. They simply provided qualitative descriptions for specific areas. Climatologists at universities were typically members of the geography department. Departments of atmospheric science did not exist. As a result, local weather forecasters had little information to work with.

Early weather observatories were relatively crude compared to the advanced scientific equipment used today.

Weather forecasts were crude and usually based on the weather of past years. Storm tracking was accomplished by telegraph, and weather forecasts were often wrong.

Meteorology and climatology were not considered serious sciences. A talented amateur was as likely to predict the weather accurately as a PhD in meteorology. In fact, few people employed by the US Weather Bureau even had college degrees. However, new discoveries in other scientific fields would soon change the stagnant field of climatology into the sophisticated atmospheric science of the late 1900s and early 2000s.

Climate and Earth's Orbit

Earth's axis tilts approximately 23.5 degrees from vertical, resulting in seasonal changes as it orbits around the sun. The North Pole points toward the sun during summer and away from the sun during winter. However, this tilt is not constant. It varies from 22.1 to 24.5 degrees over a cycle of 41,000 years.[4] Earth also undergoes a precession cycle of 22,000 years, which occurs because Earth's orbit is not perfectly circular.[5] The cycle causes variations in Earth's distance from the sun over time.

In the 1920s and 1930s, Serbian astronomer Milutin Milankovitch did complex calculations involving measurements of star positions and the effects of gravity on planets and stars. His calculations took into account both the wobble in Earth's tilt and the precession cycle. He thought this combination of cycles explained long-term climate changes, particularly ice ages. He published his ideas in 1924. However, geologists already had an accepted sequence for the timing of ice ages. Milankovitch's calculations did not match it, so they dismissed his theory.

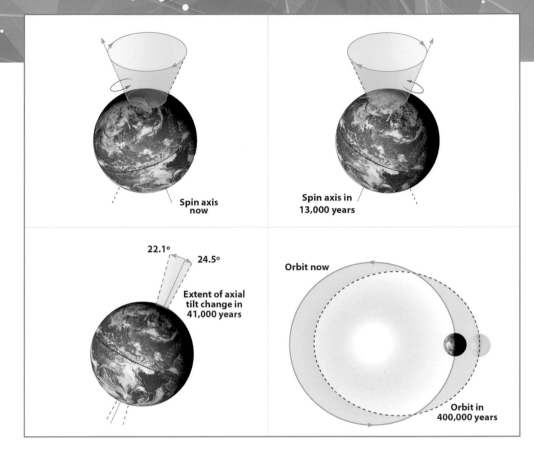

Labels within figure:
Spin axis now

Spin axis in 13,000 years

22.1° 24.5° Extent of axial tilt change in 41,000 years

Orbit now

Orbit in 400,000 years

Cycles of variation in Earth's motion have powerful effects on the planet's climate.

Proof of Milankovitch's theory had to wait several decades, until appropriate testing techniques became available. One major advance was radiocarbon dating of organic materials, developed in the 1950s. This technology made it possible to accurately date an object by studying its carbon atoms. Also, a new proxy measurement of past temperatures was discovered. It involved analyzing oxygen isotopes in fossil seashells. Italian graduate student Cesare Emiliani performed this groundbreaking work at the University of Chicago. Finally, in the 1960s, analysis of ocean sediment cores and fossil coral reefs produced additional timelines of past climate activity that matched past ice ages. Combining these more accurate timelines and temperature-proxy data, scientists were able to validate Milankovitch's theory. Long-term temperature cycles were explained by Earth's orbital and precession cycles.

The Return of Carbon Dioxide

While Milankovitch and other scientists debated the causes and timing of ice ages, meteorologists had essentially abandoned Arrhenius's idea that adding carbon dioxide to the atmosphere would increase global temperature. Scientists accepted the idea that Earth was self-regulating and that any excess carbon dioxide would be absorbed by the oceans.

But one English engineer and amateur meteorologist brought back Arrhenius's theory and provided measurements to back it up. From his home in West Sussex, Guy

Stewart Callendar obtained and analyzed worldwide weather data. He showed that both atmospheric carbon dioxide and global temperatures were rising.

In 1938, Callendar published his findings in a paper titled, "The Artificial Production of Carbon Dioxide and Its Influence on Temperature."[6] In 1957, scientists Roger Revelle and Hans Seuss referred to the "Callendar Effect," which they defined as climate change brought about by increased atmospheric carbon dioxide due to burning fossil fuels. Callendar had successfully established the notion that humans could cause climate change.

Getting Serious about Climate Science

World War II and the Cold War gave a strong boost to the science of meteorology. The military trained thousands of meteorologists, and after the war, many stayed with the navy and air force. The armed forces particularly wanted meteorologists to track the movement of radioactive debris in the atmosphere resulting from nuclear weapons. Other meteorologists obtained advanced degrees and founded their own university departments. A leading figure in training these new meteorologists was Swedish-born Carl-Gustav Rossby, who in 1942 created a department of meteorology at the University of Chicago. Rossby oversaw a transition to a new way of thinking. Rather than defining weather in terms of a specific location's latitude and longitude, scientists would consider the global movement of weather systems. Rossby saw

GREENHOUSE EFFECT ON VENUS

In 1958, telescopes on Earth first revealed that the greenhouse effect had boosted Venus's temperature significantly. Later studies showed its terrifying surface conditions. Venus, similar to Earth in size and composition, has a surface pressure 90 times that of Earth and a temperature of nearly 900 degrees Fahrenheit (480°C).[7] Its atmosphere may once have had water, but heat broke up the water molecules and their hydrogen was lost to space. Clouds of deadly sulfuric acid cloak its surface. Today, the atmosphere of Venus is 96 percent carbon dioxide, causing a runaway greenhouse effect.[8] Earth's atmosphere is only 0.038 percent carbon dioxide.[9] However, because even tiny increases in carbon dioxide lead to temperature rise, scientists worry about Earth's future greenhouse effect.

climate as dynamic, not static. Rossby's group became the first to develop climatic models that took the entire Earth into account.

In 1945, the US Office of Naval Research began funding many climate-related areas. Competition with the USSR during the Cold War led to generous government funding for many sciences. Geophysics, which had been developing throughout the 1900s, received special attention. This field included areas such as meteorology, climatology, oceanography, and terrestrial magnetism. Throughout the century, various geophysics disciplines formed cooperative groups and shared information. This culminated in 1957–1958 with the International Geophysical Year (IGY), an organized effort to carry out interdisciplinary experiments and studies. Some of these projects related to climate.

By the mid-1900s, climate science was undergoing a revolution. Scientists understood long-term climate cycles could be explained by cycles of Earth's orbit and the planet's distance from the sun. These cycles occur on a time scale of many thousands of years, and people cannot affect them. However, it was also clear that shorter-term climate

Following the International Geophysical Year, scientists designed, tested, and launched the first generation of weather satellites.

changes—those occurring over the span of decades or centuries—are affected by human activities. These activities include the emission of carbon dioxide and other greenhouse gases into the atmosphere. In other words, it was becoming clear during this time that climate is highly complex and dynamic. Climate change has several causes, and one of them is human activity.

Climate Science
HEATS UP

$$\frac{a+b}{a} = \frac{a}{b} = 1{,}618$$

In some ways, 1957 was the year modern climate science was launched. Headlines in that year featured news of the first artificial satellite, *Sputnik*, being rocketed to space by the USSR. The United States and the USSR began competing in the field of space technology. However, the IGY continued to draw funding and international cooperation to less flashy climate-related projects. In the next decade, the effect of greenhouse gases on global temperature would start to be taken seriously, and the first major attempts would be made to create mathematical models of world climate processes. Computers, which were rapidly becoming faster, smaller, and cheaper, would make these attempts much easier.

Gilbert N. Plass was a physicist who spent his spare time calculating the effects of carbon dioxide in the atmosphere. He determined in 1956 that doubling the carbon

Advances in computer technology
would soon make computers
valuable tools for climatologists.

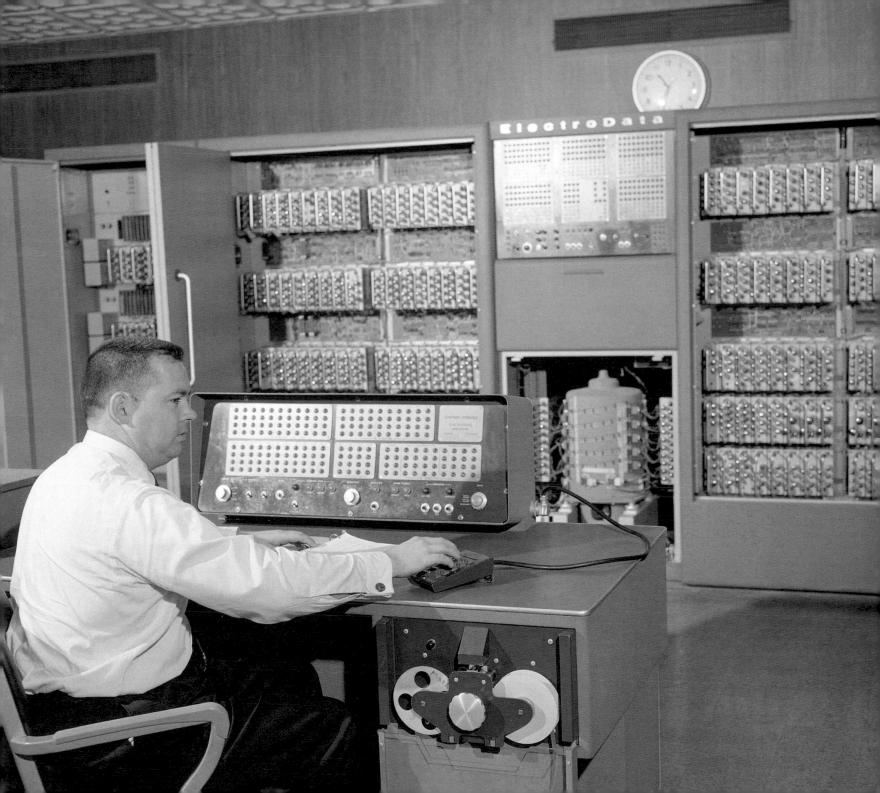

dioxide level would increase atmospheric temperatures by 5.4–7.2 degrees Fahrenheit (3–4°C); thus, if human-caused carbon dioxide emissions continued at 1950s rates, global temperatures would rise 2 degrees Fahrenheit (1.1°C) per century.[1] Plass had better data than Arrhenius or Chamberlin, so his calculations were more accurate. But he failed to consider the effects of water vapor or clouds. He also estimated that carbon dioxide would remain in the atmosphere for 1,000 years, while most scientists assumed the oceans would quickly absorb any excess. Plass was soon proven correct. Although the oceans do absorb some carbon dioxide, new measurements showed clearly that, within a few years, carbon dioxide from fossil fuel burning was thoroughly mixed throughout the atmosphere. Nevertheless, Plass incorrectly concluded that heating from an increased greenhouse effect would not be a problem for several centuries.

Tracking Carbon Dioxide

While Plass and others were making calculations, some researchers were collecting data to try to verify these calculations. Chemists Hans Seuss and Roger Revelle of the Scripps Institution of Oceanography in La Jolla, California, began measuring the ratios of different types of carbon atoms in the atmosphere and oceans over time. This allowed them to track carbon movements and determine where carbon dioxide from fossil fuels was going. They determined that oceans took up an emitted carbon dioxide molecule from the atmosphere within approximately ten years.[2] This suggested that the oceans would absorb excess carbon dioxide. However, Revelle

Revelle was among the first scientists to publish papers on the link between carbon dioxide and rising temperatures.

and Swedish meteorologists Burt Bolin and Erik Eriksson also realized that oceans have chemicals that can prevent the water from holding onto the carbon dioxide it absorbs. Most carbon dioxide actually went back into the atmosphere through evaporation, rather than into the ocean depths.

TRACKING CARBON ISOTOPES

The element carbon occurs in three isotopes. Most carbon is carbon-12. Approximately 1 percent is carbon-13, and approximately one per trillion carbon atoms on Earth is radioactive carbon-14.[5] During photosynthesis, plants mostly take in the lighter carbon-12. As a result, both modern plants and fossil fuels—which were once prehistoric plants—have slightly less carbon-13 than does the atmosphere. Carbon-14 is generated by cosmic rays in the atmosphere and decays within tens of thousands of years. Fossil fuels are made up of much older material, and therefore contain virtually no carbon-14. Long-term measurements of these isotopes help scientists determine sources of atmospheric carbon dioxide.

In the late 1950s, Plass, Revelle, Bolin, and Eriksson began to warn the public of the dangers of increasing atmospheric carbon dioxide. Bolin and Eriksson calculated that carbon dioxide would rise 25 percent by 2000, given an exponential rise in industrial production.[3] The actual measured rise between 1958 and 2000 ended up being approximately 17 percent.[4] In 1962, Russian climate expert Mikhail Budyko also predicted a drastic increase in carbon dioxide levels. These predictions received little attention. Methods for measuring carbon dioxide were still relatively primitive, and scientists were unsure of their accuracy.

The Keeling Curve

Now that scientists understood the effect of carbon dioxide on rising global temperatures, a critical question remained. Were levels of atmospheric carbon dioxide really increasing? A full 40 years before Michael Mann compiled his hockey stick graph, one scientist was committed to answering this question. This person was Charles David Keeling. He worked for Roger Revelle at the Scripps Institution of Oceanography. Beginning in 1958, during the IGY, Keeling cooperated with Revelle and Henry Wexler of the US Weather Service

The Mauna Loa Observatory has been a key center of climate research for more than half a century.

to measure carbon dioxide levels. They set up two measuring stations. One was at Mauna Loa Observatory in Hawaii and the other was in Antarctica. The Antarctica station soon closed due to lack of funding. The Mauna Loa station continues today, providing a continuous, accurate reading of atmospheric carbon dioxide levels.

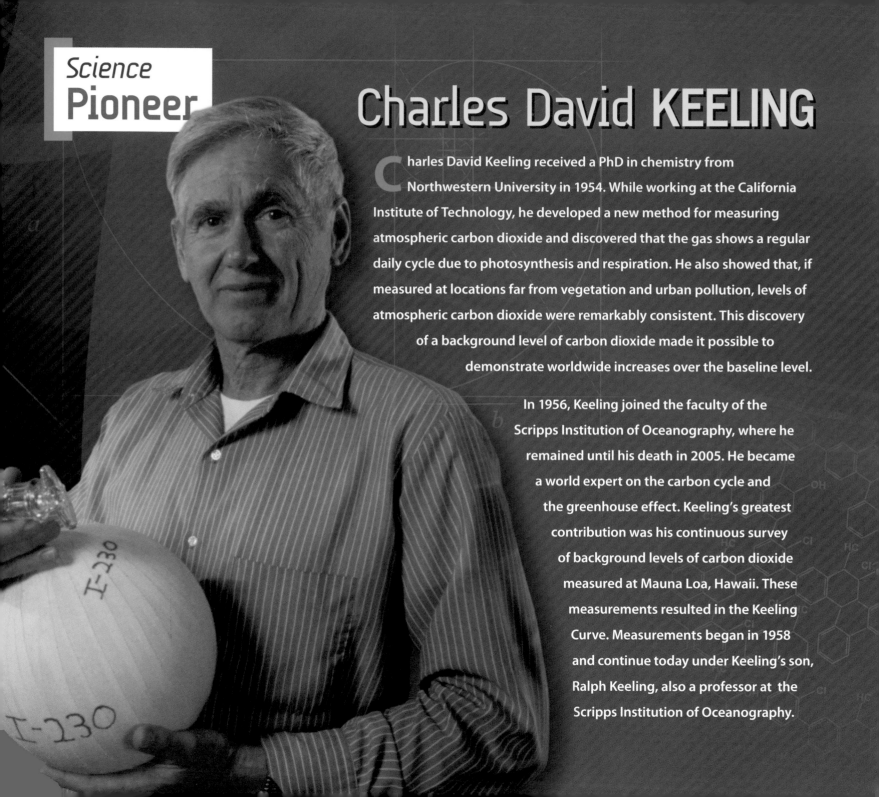

Charles David KEELING

Charles David Keeling received a PhD in chemistry from Northwestern University in 1954. While working at the California Institute of Technology, he developed a new method for measuring atmospheric carbon dioxide and discovered that the gas shows a regular daily cycle due to photosynthesis and respiration. He also showed that, if measured at locations far from vegetation and urban pollution, levels of atmospheric carbon dioxide were remarkably consistent. This discovery of a background level of carbon dioxide made it possible to demonstrate worldwide increases over the baseline level.

In 1956, Keeling joined the faculty of the Scripps Institution of Oceanography, where he remained until his death in 2005. He became a world expert on the carbon cycle and the greenhouse effect. Keeling's greatest contribution was his continuous survey of background levels of carbon dioxide measured at Mauna Loa, Hawaii. These measurements resulted in the Keeling Curve. Measurements began in 1958 and continue today under Keeling's son, Ralph Keeling, also a professor at the Scripps Institution of Oceanography.

The Mauna Loa carbon dioxide readings resulted in a graph called the Keeling Curve, climate science's first dramatic illustration of the effects of human activity on the atmosphere. The curve is typically represented by two lines: a jagged line showing seasonal variations and a second, smoother line showing yearly averages. It answered the question, "Are atmospheric carbon dioxide levels really increasing?" with a resounding yes. The Mauna Loa observatory, along with most of the world's vegetation, is in the Northern Hemisphere.

Because plants absorb carbon dioxide as part of photosynthesis, scientists would expect a seasonal zigzag variation in the data. The presence of this variation in the data suggested the data was sensitive and accurate. Since Keeling's work began, approximately 100 sites around the world have collected measurements confirming his results.[6]

Keeling developed a precise method to determine the total amount of carbon dioxide emitted by global fossil fuel consumption. He also developed an equation to calculate the percentage of fossil fuel emissions that remain in the atmosphere compared to the total amount released annually. This percentage, known as the airborne fraction (AF), has either remained relatively constant at 42 percent or

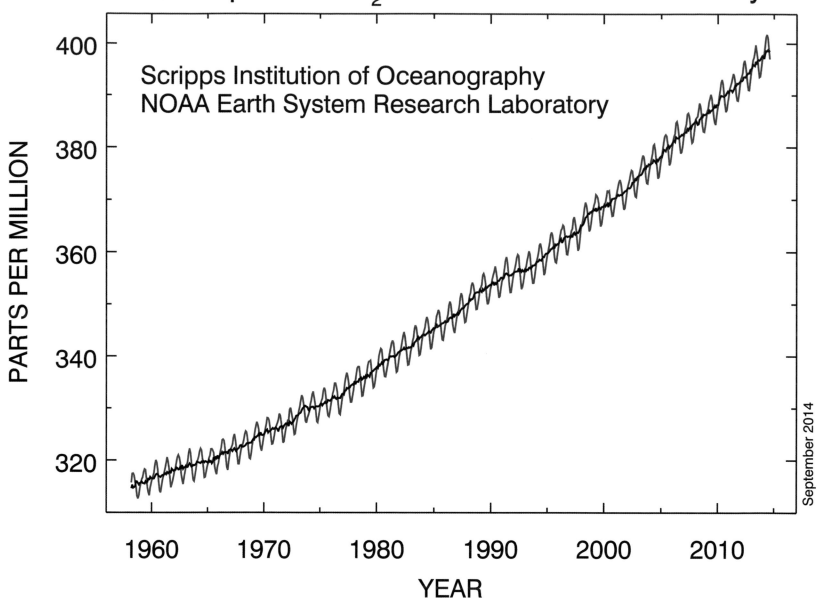

Atmospheric CO_2 at Mauna Loa Observatory

Scripps Institution of Oceanography
NOAA Earth System Research Laboratory

September 2014

increased slightly from approximately 40 to 45 percent over the last 50 years.[7] There are currently many uncertainties in this measurement, and scientists are continuing to refine their data analyses to obtain more accurate information.

The evidence presented by the Keeling Curve meant scientists could no longer deny the amount of carbon dioxide entering the atmosphere every year was greater than the amount leaving. It was also clear the oceans were not absorbing all of the excess. The debate shifted. Before, scientists argued whether carbon dioxide was rising. Now, they debated how the rise was likely to affect global climate.

Researchers Come Together

During the 1960s, global measurements gave researchers information to plug into the first tentative models of circulation of gases through the atmosphere and ecosystems. They began to unravel the pathways by which carbon, nitrogen, and other elements moved through air, water, soil, and organisms. Scientists tried to determine how much fossil fuel–produced carbon dioxide ended up in the oceans or in vegetation. The complexity of these studies

The Keeling Curve helped bring attention to the rise of global carbon dioxide levels.

THE AIRBORNE FRACTION

The airborne fraction (AF) is the fraction of human-generated carbon dioxide that remains in the atmosphere. It is the ratio of atmospheric carbon dioxide increase in a given year to that year's total carbon dioxide emissions. Carbon dioxide emissions initially enter the atmosphere, but some of the gas quickly dissolves in the oceans and some enters land sinks (soils, rocks, and forests). Percentages entering each sink vary from year to year, due to climate variations, volcanic eruptions, and other factors. A rise in AF could occur if carbon sinks, such as oceans, become saturated and unable to absorb more carbon dioxide or if carbon emissions grow faster than sinks can absorb them. Both appear to be happening.

EDWARD LORENZ: A NEW BREED OF METEOROLOGIST

Edward Lorenz was a mathematician when the US Army Air Corps made him a weather forecaster during World War II. After the war, he obtained a PhD in meteorology at the Massachusetts Institute of Technology, where he later became a professor and department chair. He is well known for his contributions to chaos theory, and he coined the term *butterfly effect*. The idea is that a butterfly flapping its wings in one part of the world may set off a chain of interactions that eventually leads to a hurricane in another part of the world. In other words, tiny changes in the initial conditions of a system can lead to dramatic and unexpected consequences.

led to new collaborations among researchers. Ecologists studying the movement of various elements through plants and animals worked with geochemists and oceanographers. Model designers worked with computer specialists. Still, most scientists were not overly concerned about the global warming impacts of excess carbon dioxide.

Then, during a 1965 meeting in Boulder, Colorado, scientists discussed causes of climate change. Edward Lorenz of the Massachusetts Institute of Technology presented his computer simulations of climate, which suggested very small differences in initial conditions, such as temperature or carbon dioxide levels, could cause drastic changes in future climate outcomes. This observation formed the basis for his chaos theory, the idea that tiny changes in highly complex systems can have huge impacts over a long period of time. His work suggested Earth was vulnerable to sudden shifts in climate. In 1967, an international organization, the Global Atmospheric Research Program (GARP), was set up to study and improve weather forecasting. Rising carbon dioxide levels were now generally accepted, and GARP included climate study as part of its goal.

Carbon dioxide emissions were confirmed as a key contributor to global warming by the mid-1960s.

Climate researchers were finally realizing the importance of carbon dioxide in present and future climate. They were beginning serious efforts to research its effects and were banding together to do it. Climate science was heating up.

The Rise of
ATMOSPHERIC SCIENCE

$$\frac{a+b}{a} = \frac{a}{b} = 1,618$$

By the late 1960s, scientists still had little understanding of the exact processes that drove climate variation. They were not even certain whether the climate was warming or cooling. Despite rising carbon dioxide levels, weather statistics from the 1940s and 1950s showed a slight decline in global temperatures. Some believed the cooling trend might result from human-caused pollution that blocked the sun's light. Some members of the mass media even predicted a new ice age.

Despite the confusion, a revolution in climate science was underway. In 1970, the United States created the National Oceanic and Atmospheric Administration (NOAA) to oversee the nation's climate research. This organization reflected scientists' new understanding that many factors influenced climate. Changes in Earth's orbit and astronomical cycles controlled long-term cycles, but smaller influences could cause

By the late 1960s, astronauts and satellites could see Earth from high above, but the processes that drove its clouds remained unclear.

dramatic climate shifts in the short term. Natural causes included volcanic eruptions, variations in sunlight, and ocean circulation patterns. Human causes included burning fossil fuels, which added both smoke particles that could cause cooling and greenhouse gases that could cause warming. Deforestation and agriculture also had effects, although no one was quite sure what they might be. More and better weather data was constantly fed into increasingly sophisticated climate modeling computer programs, and answers slowly began emerging.

More Carbon Dioxide Evidence

The Mauna Loa measurements continued showing rising carbon dioxide levels. Other scientists tried to determine where the excess human-caused carbon dioxide was going. In addition to the atmosphere and oceans, considerable carbon dioxide was found to cycle through forests and their soils.

First collected in the 1960s, information from ice cores finally led scientists to accept the correlation between carbon dioxide levels and global temperatures. Ice cores hold tiny pockets of air from the time the ice was formed. Cores from both Greenland and Antarctica showed that, during ice ages, carbon dioxide levels fell as much as 50 percent below their levels in warmer times.[1] A 1985 study of a core from Antarctica revealed a 150,000-year record showing temperature cycles from warmth to ice age and back to warmth. Carbon dioxide levels followed temperature cycles very closely, strongly supporting the relationship between carbon dioxide and

Collecting ice cores from Antarctica provided additional evidence for Earth's carbon history.

EXTRACTING ICE CORES

Massive ice sheets have accumulated snow and ice for millions of years. Ice cores are cylinders of ice a few inches in diameter that are drilled from an ice sheet. Placing these cylinders end to end reveals the history of the ice sheet. Air pockets trapped within the cores contain gases present in the atmosphere when that ice was deposited. During the Greenland Ice Sheet Project 2, a major ice core drilling project undertaken by the United States in the early 1990s, two drilling crews drilled day and night. Scientists prepared the cores for shipping back to the laboratory in Denver, Colorado. During five summers, drillers produced two miles (3.2 km) of cores.[5] They revealed a climate record stretching back more than 100,000 years.[6]

temperature rise. Eventually, core data reached back 400,000 years, covering four complete glacial cycles. Carbon dioxide levels dropped to 180 parts per million (ppm) during ice ages and rose to 280 ppm during warm periods.[2] For comparison, levels in the air in 2005 were 378 ppm. According to the most recent ice core data, this is higher than any time in at least the last 650,000 years.[3] In April 2014, levels reached 402 ppm.[4]

Other Greenhouse Gases

In the 1970s and 1980s, scientists began to realize carbon dioxide and water vapor were not the only important greenhouse gases. Other heat-absorbing gases were present in quantities measurable in parts per billion (ppb). Because their amounts were so tiny, most scientists assumed they would not affect climate. Finally, they recognized these gases could be much more potent per molecule than carbon dioxide. Minor industrial chemicals called chlorofluorocarbons (CFCs) were at first assumed to be harmless because of their small quantities. But the gases were able to remain in the atmosphere for centuries without

Raising large herds of livestock can release an enormous amount of methane into the atmosphere.

changing. One CFC molecule may absorb 10,000 times more heat than one carbon dioxide molecule.[7]

Another greenhouse gas, at first considered too minor to worry about, is one of the most serious. This gas is methane. It is produced naturally in wetlands, rice paddies, soil bacteria, and cattle intestines. In the 1980s, atmospheric methane levels rose 11 percent.[8] Over a century, each methane molecule in the atmosphere traps 30 times more heat than each carbon dioxide molecule.[9] As air temperatures warm, methane is released from two sources. Clathrates are ice-like substances that trap methane compounds. They are found in seabed sediments around the world. Permafrost is frozen soil in the Arctic. Both release methane as they melt, so a warming planet can boost emissions of the gas dramatically. Methane emissions increased by at least 20 percent between 1970 and 2000.[10] A 2005 study suggested methane is an even more powerful greenhouse gas than previously estimated.

The Climate from Space

When the United States began launching satellites and other spacecraft in the 1960s, scientists quickly realized space-based monitoring equipment could provide a complete view of Earth's weather. Such equipment could also provide long-term, cumulative climate data. Since then, weather and climate satellite programs have proliferated. They now involve cooperation among the US National Aeronautics and Space Administration (NASA), NOAA, Europe, Russia, and Japan.

NASA is primarily responsible for the Earth Observing System, a series of 17 separate space programs that collect weather and climate data. Terra and Aqua satellites measure fine particles in the atmosphere called aerosols. The Aura satellite studies ozone concentrations. The GRACE and ICESat missions study changes in Earth's ice sheets. The OSTM/Jason-2 and Jason-1 missions record the rate of sea level rise. In addition, new weather instruments are greatly improving weather and storm forecasting. NASA also obtains and analyzes data from NOAA satellites and space agencies in other countries.

NOAA manages two types of satellites. Some of these are launched into geostationary orbits. They orbit Earth at the same speed the planet rotates. This means they remain above a constant point on Earth's surface. A series of geostationary satellites located at specific points around Earth's equator provides views of a large part of Earth. Polar-orbiting satellites move in south-to-north orbits, from pole to pole. Satellites in both types of orbit monitor and help predict many different weather, climate, and environmental events.

By the late 1980s, scientists considered climate change a serious issue and were developing sophisticated methods for collecting climate data. In addition to the satellites, international interdisciplinary research groups were formed. Research budgets doubled and tripled as governments around the world began their own national initiatives to study climate change. The urgency built as evidence for global warming mounted and temperatures in the 1970s and 1980s began a rapid and unprecedented rise.

GLOBAL WARMING POTENTIAL

A greenhouse gas present in very small quantities can have drastic impacts on temperature, depending on its lifetime in the atmosphere and its heat-trapping efficiency. Both CFCs and nitrous oxide trap heat more efficiently and stay in the environment much longer than carbon dioxide. Methane stays in the atmosphere a much shorter time than carbon dioxide, but over a century, its effect on global warming is still more than 20 times greater than that of carbon dioxide.[11] More than 60 percent of atmospheric methane is currently the result of human activities.[12]

NOAA's Climate Satellite Systems

The National Oceanic and Atmospheric Administration currently runs several satellite missions:

+ The Polar Operational Environmental Satellites make 14 polar orbits per day. They enable five-to-ten-day weather predictions, long-term climate research and prediction, and measurements including atmospheric temperature, humidity, and ocean dynamics.

+ The Geostationary Operational Environmental Satellites (GOES) take photographs every 15 minutes to identify storms and other weather phenomena in the Northern Hemisphere. The first GOES-R satellite, representing the next generation of weather satellites, will launch in 2016, followed by other launches in 2017, 2019, and 2024. The updated instruments of the R-series will track hurricanes and measure interactions among land, ocean, atmosphere, and climate processes.

+ The Ocean Surface Topography Mission is a joint operation with NASA and two European agencies to monitor worldwide sea surface heights, which are needed to study ocean circulation, climate change, and sea level rise.

+ The Joint Polar Satellite System (JPSS) will collect data critical for weather forecasting and climate measurements. This set of satellites will also include instruments to measure radiation and ozone levels. The first satellite was scheduled to launch in 2016.

The GOES-R satellite system is a collaboration between NOAA and NASA.

Chapter Six

Evidence for WARMING BUILDS

$$\frac{a+b}{a} = \frac{a}{b} = 1,618$$

In 1988, a major shift changed the public understanding of climate science. Scientists already had a clear understanding of greenhouse gases, and they understood human activities were causing rising atmospheric carbon dioxide levels. They knew global temperatures were rising and were likely to rise another 2 degrees Fahrenheit (1°C) or more in the coming century.[1] They continued to develop better models, collect more complete and precise data, and consider possible sources of change.

However, US media coverage of climate issues so far had been lukewarm and sporadic. In November 1987, NASA climate scientist James Hansen told a congressional committee, "The global warming predicted in the next 20 years will make the Earth warmer than it has been in the past 100,000 years."[2] His statement

Melting glaciers and other visible signs of climate change made the danger of a warming planet more evident.

James HANSEN

James Hansen is one of the most colorful and controversial figures in the climate change field. Hansen attended the University of Iowa, receiving a BA in physics and mathematics with highest distinction, an MS in astronomy, and a PhD in physics. He spent his entire career at NASA's Goddard Institute for Space Studies in New York City and was an adjunct professor at nearby Columbia University.

Hansen began his career studying Venus's greenhouse effect but quickly switched to analyzing human impacts on Earth's climate. As evidence for climate change mounted, he became an outspoken activist. His 1988 testimony before Congress brought climate change to public attention. But climate change deniers consider him an alarmist, and some scientific colleagues worry his activism limits his scientific credibility. In 2013, Hansen retired from NASA to devote himself full-time to climate change activism.

received little attention. But he testified in Congress again in June 1988, stating "with 99 percent confidence" that the warming trend was long-term and likely caused by the greenhouse effect.[3] He predicted increases in global temperatures would become obvious by 2000. This time, the media and the public listened. Many scientists, however, felt Hansen had gone too far. Many were also upset by exaggerations and inaccuracies in media reports about climate change.

Nations Come Together

In 1988, only a year after a successful agreement known as the Montreal Protocol set standards for eliminating CFCs, a group of scientists and a few government representatives convened at the Toronto Conference. They set a goal for reducing worldwide greenhouse gas emissions. Specifically, they wanted greenhouse gas emissions in 2005 to be 20 percent lower than in 1988.[4] This goal followed the same principle as in Montreal: set a world standard and let each government decide how to meet it. Unfortunately, the group had little political influence. The Toronto Protocol was not successful. In 2005, greenhouse gas emissions were considerably higher than in 1988.

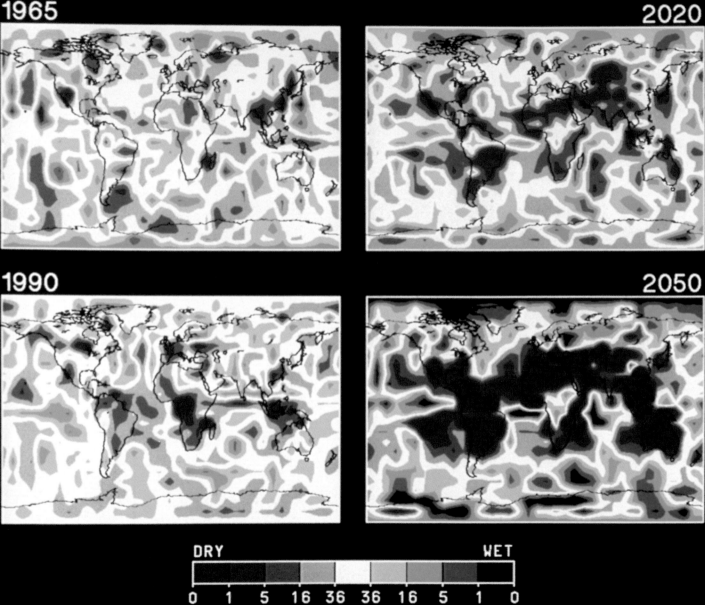

	1965	2020
	1990	2050

DRY   WET

0   1   5   16   36   36   16   5   1   0

Because climate was a worldwide phenomenon, governments saw the need for an international body with more influence to oversee climate change information. The World Meteorological Organization (WMO) and United Nations Environment Programme (UNEP) worked with the United States and other governments to create the Intergovernmental Panel on Climate Change (IPCC) in 1988. This hybrid body included both scientists and government representatives. Nearly all of the world's climate scientists associated themselves with the IPCC, which began producing periodic reports on the state of the world climate.

Climate Models and Decadal Shifts

As the world organized and became aware of climate change, scientists continued finding evidence. Climate models became better at reproducing actual climatic changes. Modelers used data collected by paleontologists on ancient climates to validate their models' reliability. A model that reliably reproduced past climates could be used to predict future climates with reasonable accuracy.

Also, studies of pollen grains and other climate proxy data were showing that climate was not stable over many thousands of years, as was previously thought. It included stable periods, particularly on a regional scale, punctuated by quick climate shifts that occurred in just a century or two. Deep-sea sediment and ice core data reinforced the accuracy of these relatively rapid shifts. During the 1990s, American and European teams drilled two separate holes 19 miles (30 km) apart through the

Climate models are used to predict the future spread of dangerous climate events, such as droughts.

SETTING CLIMATE RECORDS

The year 1998 was the hottest year since reliable records had been kept. The record has since been surpassed several times. The mean land surface temperature in 1998 was 58.1 degrees Fahrenheit (14.5°C), or 1.20 degrees Fahrenheit (0.55°C) above the long-term average, surpassing the previous record set in 1997.[7] Record temperatures were especially high in the tropics (1.84 degrees Fahrenheit [1°C] above average) and in the Northern Hemisphere (2.16 degrees Fahrenheit [1.20°C] above average).[8] Six extreme climate events in the United States each caused more than $1 billion in damages: a Northeastern ice storm, severe weather and tornadoes in the Southeast, a drought and heat wave in the South, flooding in Texas, and Hurricanes Bonnie and Georges.[9]

Greenland Ice Sheet.[6] Using two separate sources of data gave the scientists a way to check their findings. Any change occurring in both cores represented a real climate change, not an accident or artifact of drilling. Data showed that climate could change within one to five years—very abrupt on normal climate time scales. Separate evidence showed that these changes had occurred throughout the Northern Hemisphere. Data from ice cores in Antarctica further reinforced the idea of rapid and drastic temperature shifts. This evidence of abrupt temperature shifts worried scientists. Could such changes happen in the future?

Climate Controversies Intensify

As climate change evidence mounted, those who denied its existence became more vocal. Politicians, business leaders, and economists were less worried about climate change itself than about the effect of laws to control carbon dioxide emissions on business and the economy. Publication of the hockey stick graph in 1999 led to sometimes vicious attacks. Most attacks reflected ignorance or misinterpretation of climate science. Some detractors confused short-term weather variations with long-term trends or regional changes with global changes. Others insisted the authors made errors or used invalid statistics to calculate temperatures from proxy data, even though other scientists had validated their methods.

Another serious attack by climate change deniers occurred as the result of an incident at the University of East Anglia (UEA) in the United Kingdom. The university is home to a small but important climate science group, the Climatic Research Unit (CRU). In November 2009, the CRU's computers were hacked. Thieves stole 1,079 emails and 72 documents and published them on the Internet.[10] The internal emails included 13 years of correspondence among colleagues at UEA and outside scientists. Although most of the stolen emails were routine, a few led opponents to accuse the scientists of manipulating data to support predetermined conclusions, refusing to show their data, and corrupting the IPCC and quality review processes.

Several separate investigations showed that the scientists had not falsified climate data or bypassed proper scientific processes. However, although the initial incident was widely covered in the press, the investigations that cleared the scientists of wrongdoing were not. Many people continue to

Who Stole the Emails?

One factor was almost ignored during the Climategate scandals: who stole the emails and why? In July 2012, local police closed a 2.5-year investigation with no results. The lead detective stated that the data breach involved a "sophisticated and carefully orchestrated attack on the CRU's data files, carried out remotely via the Internet."[11] He said it would be impossible to identify the offenders and launch criminal proceedings.

In recent decades, an increasing number of protesters have called for governments to take action against climate change.

assume they falsified data. They use this as a reason to ignore or mistrust all data from all climate scientists.

Much Talk, Little Action

Over the last several decades, the United States has consistently limited its cooperation with world bodies such as the United Nations on climate change issues. A 1992 conference in Rio de Janeiro resulted in the United Nations Framework Convention on Climate Change (UNFCCC). Its objective was to limit emissions of six greenhouse gases to prevent "dangerous human interference with the climate system."[12] The 1997 Kyoto Protocol amended the UNFCCC by setting binding standards for limiting emissions. The United States objected that the protocol did not require developing countries to limit emissions. The Kyoto Protocol went into effect in 2005, ratified by 141 nations but not the United States.[13]

Successive international climate conferences have adopted agreements, but none have had much success. In December 2009, the Copenhagen Accord recognized the need to limit global greenhouse gas emissions but included no binding emission targets. By the January 2010 deadline, 141 nations, including the United States and the 37-member European Union, had associated themselves with the accord.[14] Discussion continues, but so far action has been limited.

AN INCONVENIENT TRUTH

In 2006, the documentary film *An Inconvenient Truth*, directed by Davis Guggenheim, made its international premiere at the Cannes Film Festival. It later won an Academy Award for best documentary film. The film described former vice president Al Gore's crusade to galvanize the public into action on global warming. It included facts and predictions about global warming and climate change. Some people criticized the film for having scientific errors, but experts described the film as "broadly accurate" although it contained minor errors.[15] The film has helped persuade some governments, organizations, and individuals worldwide to act on global warming.

The Rise of CLIMATE MODELING

$$\frac{a+b}{a} = \frac{a}{b} = 1.618$$

Some people, including many politicians, often see climate models as irrelevant or useless. They do not understand how models are constructed, how accurate they are, and how useful they can be. Climate scientist Gavin Schmidt points out that climate models are the best method we have for understanding climate causes and effects and predicting future climates. Scientists Tom Knutson and Robert Tuleya comment wryly, "If we had observations of the future, we would obviously trust them more than models, but unfortunately observations of the future are not available at this time."[1]

A model is a simplified representation of a real-life system. Scientists often use models when a system is too large and complex to study as a whole. They might manipulate and analyze a scale model of a spacecraft before actually building it.

Over the last few decades, computers have become powerful enough to generate accurate, detailed models of global climate.

WHO USES CLIMATE MODELS?

Many people use short-term weather forecasting models and longer-term climate models.

+ Farmers use weather forecasts to determine when to plant, irrigate, or harvest, and they use climate models to help plan future crops and equipment investments.

+ City mayors plan for natural disasters and develop long-term strategies to deal with coming climate changes.

+ Energy managers determine the amount of electricity needed for heating and cooling in a region. Water managers determine the likelihood of floods or amount of water storage needed.

+ National security planners need weather and climate knowledge to plan and execute military operations. The navy is currently planning for the effects of sea-level rise on near-shore installations.

Processes can also be modeled. A computer model simulating traffic patterns can determine the most efficient timing of stoplights. A flight simulator can help a pilot learn to fly in safety before taking the controls of a real aircraft. The model functions approximately as the real system functions. It can be manipulated in ways not possible in the actual system.

The first serious steps toward a climate model came in the late 1940s. Meteorologist Jule Charney developed equations to model climate that were simple enough for his era's computers to process, yet were complete enough to provide somewhat realistic results. The model simulated only a limited geographic area, however. Japanese scientist Syukuro Manabe developed one of the earliest global climate models in 1965. The model showed promise, but the lack of computer power meant it could only roughly approximate climate dynamics. It was unable to simulate the finer details of climate changes. As computers got faster over the next several decades, the results provided by climate models became more accurate.

The size and complexity of climate models require not only powerful computers but also the storage of vast amounts of data.

Climate Models: What Are They?

Earth's climate is among the most complex systems we experience. Climate models are based on two areas of study. The first is fluid mechanics, or the science of air movement. The second is thermodynamics, or the science of heat transfer.

Climate Supercomputers

In 2002, in Yokohama, Japan, a computer complex opened that contained 640 machines (nodes) with 16 gigabytes (16 billion bytes) of memory per node. Its job was to simulate world climate. The Earth Simulator did 35 trillion calculations per second and simulated 20 to 40 years of global climate change per day.[2] In comparison, the Blue Sky supercomputer owned by the National Center for Atmospheric Research in Boulder, Colorado, did only 8.3 trillion calculations per second and simulated four to five years of climate per day using the same climate model.[3] In 2009, Japan replaced its powerhouse computer with Earth Simulator 2. This more efficient version has only 160 nodes and does 131 trillion, instead of 35 trillion, calculations per second.[4]

Supercomputers must run nonstop for weeks at a time, doing billions of calculations to simulate the interaction of all factors affecting climate. Computer models divide Earth's surface into grid cells and contain specific climate data for each cell. The smaller the cells are, the greater resolution the model has and the more accurate it will be. For example, in the late 1990s, climate models treated the western United States as a single uniform landmass (one huge grid cell). The models could not simulate the effects of mountains, deserts, or waterways. New versions have much smaller 3.86-square-mile (10 sq km) grid cells, and even newer models will have 0.77-square-mile (2 sq km) squares. Every improvement in detail improves the model's accuracy, but it also requires much more computing power.

When it was built, the Earth Simulator was the fastest supercomputer in the world.

PARAMETRIZATION IN CLIMATE MODELS

Many climate processes occur on scales of time and space that are too small to fit the resolution of climate models. For example, clouds under different conditions can either heat or cool the atmosphere. But clouds are too small to be represented adequately in a climate model. Modelers deal with such factors by using the process of parametrization. Parametrization simplifies problems to make them easier to solve. Rather than modeling each cloud, they calculate an average value to represent the factor within each geographic segment of the model. Other factors represented by parametrization values include topography of Earth's surface and reflectivity of Earth. Better parametrizations have greatly improved climate models in the past 15 years.

The more precisely a modeler can describe these processes in the atmosphere, the more accurate a climate model will be. But climate also involves the interactions of the atmosphere, oceans, living things, ice and snow, and rocks and soils. All of these factors constantly change, and human activities further complicate the process. Thus, a good climate model encompasses thousands of actions and interactions. Each is described by one or more mathematical equations. All equations are translated into computer code, and the starting conditions are loaded into the model. The computer generates a simulated climate for a set number of years, based on the starting data. The many detailed calculations required by complex climate models mean they are usually run on supercomputers.

The same models may be used for both weather and climate forecasting. Weather forecasting must be very accurate for a given region over a short time period. It uses shorter time intervals than climate forecasting. In contrast, climate forecasts do not need to be accurate on a day-to-day basis. They predict average weather, or changes over decades or even centuries.

Older models included only interactions within the atmosphere. Newer models are much more accurate because they also include ocean processes and interactions between the oceans and atmosphere. The ocean controls the flow of heat and water vapor into the atmosphere and stores large amounts of both heat and carbon dioxide.

Validating a Climate Model

In statistical analysis, two measures, reliability and validity, are used to test a model. A model is reliable if it produces consistent, stable, and repeatable results. It is valid if it accurately measures what it is supposed to measure. A good climate model should accurately reproduce the actual climate.

Modelers test and validate climate models in several ways. First, they might run the model to simulate current stable climate conditions for many years into the future. To do this, they eliminate factors known to change the climate, such as increases in solar radiation or greenhouse gases. If they remove these factors and the model maintains a stable climate far into the future, the model is reliable and valid—that is, it mimics the natural climate very closely.

Second, they test the model by trying to reproduce climate changes observed in the past. This method has provided evidence for human effects on climate in the recent past. Initial climate values—say, climatic factors that existed in 1900—are entered into the model. Then, known changes, such as greenhouse gas levels or historical volcanic eruptions, are added. If the model reproduces temperature and

Climate models can be tested by comparing their output with proxy data, including information about past climates from tree rings.

precipitation values that actually occurred, this validates the model. The closer the fit between actual and predicted climate, the more reliable and valid the model is.

Finally, modelers validate climate models by testing them against ancient climates determined from proxy data. Although these data are less reliable than more recent data obtained from instrument measurements, climate models have accurately reproduced changes occurring in past times. One example is the southward advance of the Sahara Desert during the past 9,000 years.[5]

A model can be used to predict future climates only after it has passed many validity tests. Increases in greenhouse gases are known to cause climate change, so scientists test predictions of different levels of carbon dioxide or other greenhouse gases. These levels are based on estimates of how economic and social factors will change. Because it is very difficult to determine these changes, predictions of future climates always contain some degree of uncertainty. Predictions are typically given as ranges, rather than as definite values. For example, the fifth IPCC report in 2014 estimated that temperature increase as the carbon dioxide level doubles from its preindustrial level would be in the range of 3–8 degrees Fahrenheit (1.5–4.5°C).[6]

FUTURE CLIMATE MODELS

Climate modelers hope to develop more precise and reliable ways to simulate the effects of human-caused warming. Early models could predict a final temperature after a given rise in carbon dioxide, but they could not predict temperature changes through time. Combining ocean and atmosphere models enabled the simulation of slow ocean warming, making this possible. New models are beginning to include warming due to methane, nitrous oxide, and other greenhouse gases, as well as effects of aerosols and dust particles. Increased model accuracy also depends on increasing computer power and model resolution.

Climate Change
TODAY

$$\frac{a+b}{a} = \frac{a}{b} = 1{,}618$$

I n the late 1980s, NASA scientist James Hansen's climate model correctly predicted the warming that occurred a decade later. In 1991, after Mount Pinatubo erupted in the Philippines, Hansen added information on volcanic aerosols to his simulations and correctly predicted several years of temporary cooling after the eruption. A graph from another modeling study by climate scientist Ben Santer and colleagues in the mid-1990s shows such clear proof of the human impact on global temperatures that climate scientists call it the "smoking gun."[1]

Climate in the Early 2000s

But in the second decade of the 2000s, models and other sophisticated scientific data are hardly needed to observe changes in Earth's climate. Climate change has become hard to ignore because it is happening everywhere. Snowmelt and spring are arriving

The visible changes attributed to climate change have become difficult to ignore.

earlier. Plant communities in the Rocky Mountains are changing from wildflowers to hardier, drought-resistant sagebrush. Due to a ten-year drought, Australia's Murray River has lost so much water it no longer reaches the sea.

From 2000 through 2009, Arctic glaciers and Antarctic ice sheets melted more rapidly than climate models predicted. The Arctic ice cap reached a record low in summer 2007. The 2007 levels were themselves 22 percent below the previous record low set in 2005.[2] In 2012, the Arctic ice cap was 18 percent smaller than in 2007.[3] According to Walt Meier, scientist at the National Snow and Ice Data Center in Boulder, Colorado, "We're smashing a record that smashed a record."[4] Arctic sea ice levels are especially important because they change climate around the world. Scientists at the Boulder data center said climate models predict the Arctic could be free of summer

"THE SMOKING GUN" OF GLOBAL WARMING

The graph shows global temperatures from 1900 through 2000 with and without human influences. The black line shows measured temperatures. The pink and blue bars represent values obtained from climate models. The blue bar shows temperatures without human influences. The pink bar adds in data on greenhouse gases, which increase temperature, and aerosols from industry, which decrease it. The pink bar closely matches actual temperatures. The model even matched temperature changes region by region. Other lines of evidence had already convinced scientists of human causes, but this "smoking gun" offered final proof.

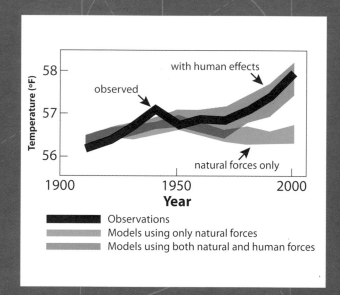

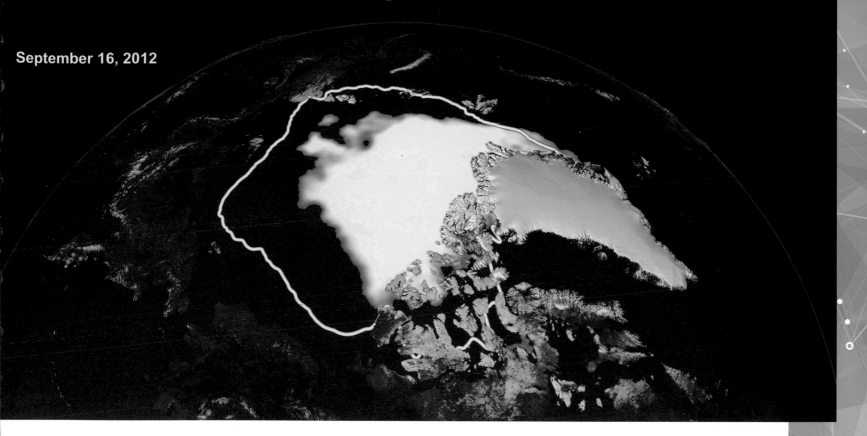

September 16, 2012

The minimum extent of summer Arctic sea ice reached a record low in September 2012. The yellow line shows the average extent for the same time of year between 1979 and 2000.

ice by 2050. However, recent trends indicate the ice continues melting even faster than the models predict.

Has Global Warming Stopped?

During the first decade of the 2000s, while global warming continued, its rate slowed slightly. That is, the angle of the graph line became flatter than it was during

EL NIÑO AND LA NIÑA

El Niño and La Niña are opposite phases of a weather cycle called the ENSO cycle. The cycle involves temperature fluctuations between the ocean and atmosphere and causes worldwide weather and climate changes. El Niño is the warm phase of the cycle; La Niña is the cold phase. Most El Niño and La Niña events last for 9 to 12 months, but some may last for years. El Niño events cause ocean temperatures in the equatorial Pacific to become unusually warm. This causes warmer temperatures in western and central Canada and the United States and higher rainfall along the Gulf Coast and in Florida.

the 1990s, when warming was very rapid. Climate change deniers have used this fact to argue that global warming—if it ever existed—has now stopped. But as scientists know, natural factors always cause slight annual and even decadal variations in global temperatures. These include cloud variability, volcanic activity, and ocean conditions. According to James Hansen, one human cause of temperature variation was an increase in pollution, such as aerosols from coal burning, from countries such as China and India.

But two natural ocean circulation patterns are most likely the major reasons atmospheric temperatures have leveled off. The first is the El Niño Southern Oscillation (ENSO) cycle in the tropical Pacific Ocean. During the past decade, a series of La Niña weather patterns, which cause atmospheric cooling, dominated the ENSO cycle. The second pattern is the Pacific Decadal Oscillation (PDO), whose phases affect climate over decades rather than years. The PDO phase since the late 1990s has caused cooler sea surface temperatures and mixed the water, moving heat 0.5 miles (0.8 km) down into the deep ocean.[5]

While air temperatures leveled off during this time, excess heat continued entering the atmosphere. The heat had to be absorbed somewhere, and most of it went into the oceans. Oceans have a much higher heat capacity than air, meaning they can absorb more heat before their temperatures begin to rise. Also, they have a huge volume in which to store heat. After 2000, ocean temperatures began rising noticeably. Shallow waters warmed slowly, but deep waters warmed much faster. Scientists expect some of this stored heat will return to the surface, increasing atmospheric temperatures, when the El Niño phase of the ENSO cycle returns.

The Years 2012–2014

Global temperatures in 2012 were 1.03 degrees Fahrenheit (0.57°C) above the 1900s average, making it the tenth-warmest year on record.[6] Total greenhouse gas emissions reached record highs according to the World Meteorological Organization. However, US greenhouse gas emissions actually decreased slightly. US emissions have been rising 0.2 percent annually since 1990, but from 2011 to 2012, they decreased 3.4 percent, to a value 10 percent below 2005 levels.[7] Reasons for the decrease included reduced power plant emissions, better auto fuel efficiency, and fewer miles traveled. In terms of weather extremes, 2012 was an average year worldwide. But almost two-thirds of the extreme events that occurred were in the United States, including Superstorm Sandy, a Midwestern drought, and severe tornadoes.

The year 2013 was the fourth warmest year on record. The year was notable for weather extremes. California and Oregon suffered record droughts. The Pacific Typhoon Haiyan was the largest tropical cyclone ever to hit land. It killed 5,700 people in the Philippines and affected 11 million people overall. After surviving a decade-long drought, Australia reached its highest-ever average temperature in 2013. Russia and China suffered extensive flooding after several severe bursts of rainfall. One township in China received half of its average annual rainfall in a single day.[8]

In early 2014, one major climate event was a symbolic milestone in carbon dioxide levels. In April 2014, the average carbon dioxide level remained above 400 ppm for the entire month. This was the highest level in 800,000 to 15 million years. Commenting on this milestone, NASA climate scientist Annmarie Eldering said, "Reaching 400ppm is a stark reminder that the world is still not on a track to limit carbon dioxide emissions and therefore climate impacts. We're still on the 'business-as-usual' path . . . which will impact the generations ahead of us."[9]

Typhoon Haiyan cannot be blamed directly on climate change, but climate change makes devastating storms more likely.

Climate Change
TOMORROW

$$\frac{a+b}{a} = \frac{a}{b} = 1.618$$

Two major climate reports were released in 2014: the fifth report of the IPCC and the latest US government National Climate Assessment. Both describe the climate situation as urgent. According to the US government, "Climate change, once considered an issue for a distant future, has moved firmly into the present."[1] The US report describes effects of climate change on infrastructure, water supplies, agriculture, disease transmission, and air quality. However, John Podesta, an adviser to President Barack Obama, says decision makers at all levels still need to be convinced. "They get that climate change is happening, they get that it is caused by human activity and support the solutions to climate change, but they don't feel that sense of urgency," Podesta said.[2]

The danger of rising sea levels is highlighted by this artist's rendition of San Francisco, California, following a 12-foot (3.7 m) rise.

HOW TO PREVENT A CATASTROPHE

The IPCC's Fifth Assessment Report states that to avoid catastrophic global warming, 2050 global greenhouse gas emissions must drop 40–70 percent below their 2010 levels.[5] Possible actions to help achieve this goal include:

1. **Switch to renewable sources of energy and phase out fossil fuels.**

2. **Place a tax on carbon emissions.**

3. **Actively remove carbon from the atmosphere.**

4. **Make buildings energy-efficient.**

5. **Plan cities for efficient use of space; use public transportation.**

6. **Require energy reduction in industry.**

7. **Require energy-efficient vehicles.**

8. **Stop deforestation; manage agricultural land sustainably.**

9. **Live individual lifestyles in ways that reduce carbon emissions.**

10. **Cooperate internationally.**

Many politicians still reject climate change entirely. Senator David Vitter, Louisiana Republican and ranking member of the Senate Environment Committee, feels acting on climate change would hurt the nation's economy. A group called the Cato Institute says the US report "overly focuses on the supposed negative impacts from climate change while largely dismissing or ignoring the positives from climate change."[3] And two weeks after the National Climate Assessment was released, the US House of Representatives voted to prevent the Department of Defense from using funds to address national security impacts of climate change.

Climate Change in the Near Future

While policymakers drag their feet, climate is changing rapidly. Within a year after National Climate Assessment data collection ended, 19 states set new individual climate records. In January 2013, no part of California was suffering extreme or exceptional drought. By early May 2014, these conditions applied to 77 percent of the state.[4]

Drought conditions in California have led to more intense wildfires that begin earlier in the year.

Michael Mann has calculated climate scenarios based on information from the recent IPCC report. He looked at the warming expected after carbon dioxide concentrations double to 560 ppm from their preindustrial level. Scientists generally consider 3.6 degrees Fahrenheit (2°C) to be a limit below which the planet will not suffer damaging effects. Mann calculated "optimistic" estimates, assuming rises of 4.5 degrees Fahrenheit (2.5°C) and 5.4 degrees Fahrenheit (3°C) as safe limits.

He found that continuing the current level of carbon emissions, we will reach the 2.5°C limit in 2036 and the 3°C limit only ten years later.[6] Both dates are well within the life-spans of most people living today.

US Climate Change Effects

Climate-induced storms, floods, and droughts make the United States' infrastructure extremely vulnerable, according to the National Climate Assessment. An impact on one piece of infrastructure can have cascading effects on others. Hurricane Katrina, for example, damaged electricity-generating power plants. There was no energy to pump oil through pipelines, and refineries could not operate. Gas prices around the country rose. Other likely situations include a storm destroying communication lines or a flood damaging a major bridge or highway. These scenarios could cause shutdowns in businesses and manufacturing, traffic backups, delays in shipment of goods, and other impacts. The resulting chaos would have profound effects on both individuals and economic systems.

Hurricane Sandy, which hit the Northeast Coast in October 2012, generated a storm tide more than four feet (1.2 m) higher than the previous record in 1992. A new study found that storm tides high enough to breach the seawall of Manhattan in New York City are now likely to happen once every four to five years. Sea levels in New York Harbor have risen 1.5 feet (0.5 m) since the mid-1800s.[7] Another study warns about impacts of abrupt climate change. Rapid ice melting may cause sea levels to rise much more quickly than anticipated. Climate changes may disrupt the lives of plants or animals, leading to extinctions or changes in crop species. The study recommends early warning systems to detect these abrupt changes.

World Climate Change Effects

Writer Joe Romm notes that the fifth IPCC report, which covers conditions over the entire world, lists a number of "reasons for concern" (RFCs) related to climate change. One RFC is "breakdown of food systems linked to warming, drought, flooding, and precipitation variability and extremes."[8] Increased food prices following climate extremes are already happening. Imagine, Romm says, the impact of adding another 2 billion people to the world while the climate warms five times as much as it did in the 1900s.

The IPCC report also concludes, "Climate change makes violent conflict more likely—and violent conflict makes a country more vulnerable to climate change."[9] When considered together, these conclusions suggest the likelihood of more wars, leading to failed states in

CLIMATE CHANGE IN THE TROPICS

The tropics have the world's highest biodiversity, but tropical organisms are adapted to very stable climates. Rapid temperature rise will speed up extinction and loss of biodiversity. The Amazon rain forest already shows changes in precipitation patterns, river levels, and temperatures. Over each decade since 1979, the dry season in the southern Amazon has increased by one week, and thus the fire season is also longer. If these conditions persist, they could eventually convert much of the southern Amazon from rain forest to savanna.

climate-vulnerable areas around the world. Romm states that because the IPCC relies on consensus, it generally includes only things on which most scientists can agree. Therefore, its conclusions tend to be very cautious. In other words, even its cautious predictions are quite severe.

Ice Sheets and Sea Level Rise

The West Antarctic Ice Sheet (WAIS) is held in place only by floating ice shelves at its rim. Anything upsetting this delicate balance causes ice shelves to break off the continent and lets the ice sheets flow. In 2014, a 40-year NASA study using ground, airplane, and satellite data showed that WAIS melting has already begun and is now "unstoppable." The warming ocean is melting the underside of the floating ice shelves. The melting is just beginning. It will cause only approximately 0.04 inches (1 mm) of sea level rise per year for the next century, after which it will accelerate.

Causes of Sea Level Rise

Two factors are responsible for sea level rise: melting of ice on land and the expansion of water as it heats. During summers, land ice melts from glaciers, polar ice caps, and the Greenland and West Antarctic Ice Sheets. Scientists estimate each factor accounts for approximately half of the rise.

Scientists describe the melting as a "slow-motion collapse." Total melting is expected to take between 200 and 900 years. The likely figure is estimated to be closer to 200.[10]

Recent discoveries about Greenland's underground topography have led researchers to conclude this ice sheet will also contribute much more to sea level rise than previously thought. Many

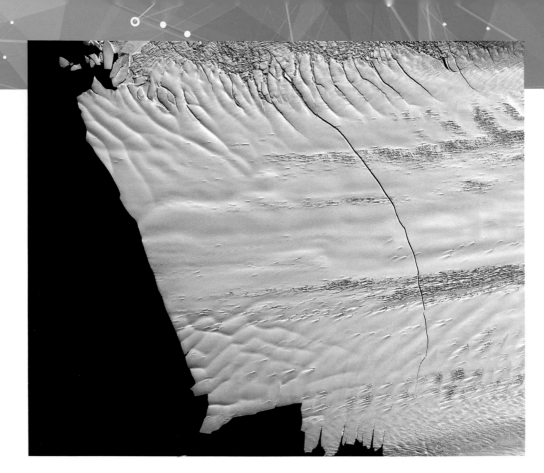

In 2011, satellite images revealed a 19-mile (31 km) crack in a glacier that drains into the WAIS.

deep, fingerlike valleys extend many miles inland under the Greenland Ice Sheet. As warmer waters from the Atlantic reach the Greenland coast, they will reach under the ice into these valleys. Melting rates will increase, and Greenland's glaciers will retreat inland faster and farther than originally expected.

In the past century, average sea levels have risen approximately four to eight inches (10 to 20 cm). Over the past 20 years, the rate of rise was double that of the previous 80 years, and the rate appears to be accelerating.[11] Even small sea-level rises have serious consequences for coastal habitats. As water reaches inland, it increases erosion, floods wetlands, contaminates aquifers and soils with salt water, and destroys habitats. Rising sea levels also mean higher storm surges and more powerful floods. Accelerating rates of melting may cause oceans to rise 2.5 to 6.5 feet (0.8 to 2.0 m) by 2100, flooding several major cities on the East Coast of the United States.[12]

How Much Warming Can Civilization Take?

Science writer Bill McKibben summarized the world's current "climate predicament" using three numbers: 3.6 degrees Fahrenheit (2°C), 565 gigatons, and 2,795 gigatons. The first number comes from the 2009 Copenhagen climate conference, which defined 3.6 degrees Fahrenheit (2°C) as the maximum allowable increase in global temperature before global damage occurs. The temperature has already risen 1.44 degrees Fahrenheit (0.8°C). The second number, 565 gigatons, is the amount of carbon dioxide that can be added to the atmosphere by 2050 to still leave a reasonable chance of keeping the temperature rise below the maximum limit. At current emission levels, the increase will exceed 565 gigatons by 2024. Finally, 2,795 gigatons is the estimated amount of unburned fossil fuel existing in proven coal, oil, and gas reserves. This amount is five times higher than the amount we can add. These numbers have been available for several decades. Yet, McKibben says, "We're in the same position we've been in for a quarter-century: scientific warning followed by political inaction."[13]

Climate Science Today and Tomorrow

Climate science began in the twentieth century as a minor science concerned only with monitoring regional weather. But since at least the 1950s, climate scientists have been aware of the effects of greenhouse gases and other human activities on Earth's climate. They have struggled to understand these effects and make them known. Today climate science is dynamic, technologically sophisticated, and focused on solving potentially catastrophic future climate change. In the future, as now, climate change research will likely focus on three areas of study: the physical processes controlling climate and the effects of continuing to add greenhouse gases, the impacts and consequences of climate change on the environment and society, and

CLIMATE ENGINEERING

Climate engineering is the large-scale artificial manipulation of Earth's climate system. This is increasingly discussed as global greenhouse gas emissions increase despite international agreements to reduce them. Researchers at the Helmholtz Centre for Ocean Research Kiel conducted a modeling study simulating climate engineering techniques, including reducing incoming solar radiation, turning the Sahara and Australian deserts into forest, and increasing ocean carbon uptake. The new, darker forests actually increased warming because they absorbed more heat. The models then showed that stopping climate engineering after a few decades caused rapid, catastrophic warming.

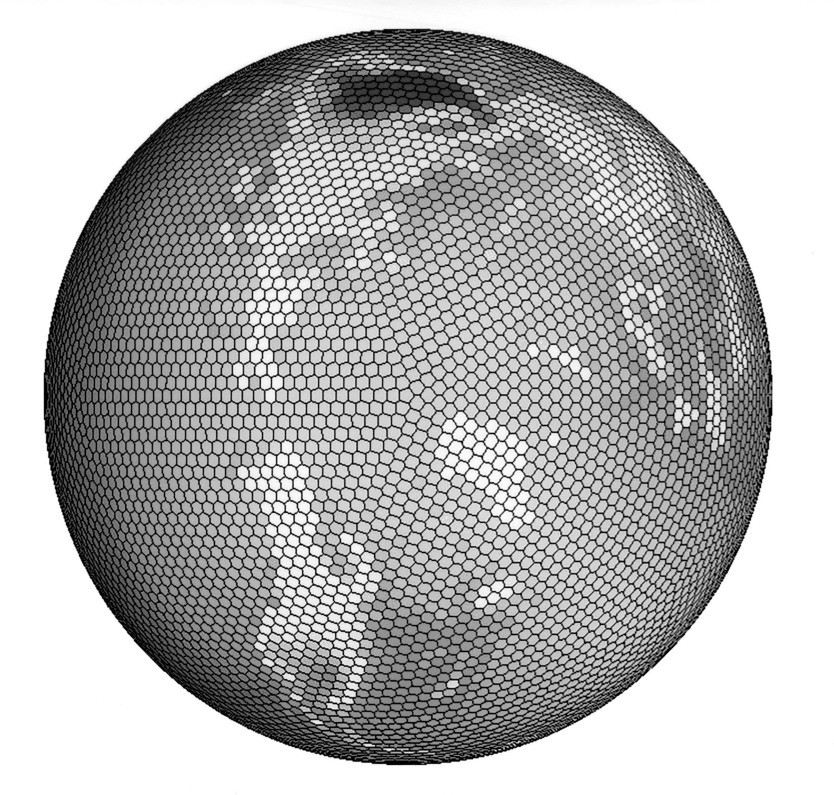

possible ways to limit further greenhouse gas emissions or remove them from the atmosphere.

One upcoming development is the improvement of climate models to incorporate cloud modeling. Under different conditions, clouds can either warm or cool the planet. Currently they have a cooling effect, but no one knows how this will change as the climate continues to warm. A new computer model, the Global Cloud Resolving Model (GCRM), attacks this problem by simulating the motion of the atmosphere. It divides the three-dimensional structure of the atmosphere into 1 billion tiny grid cells, each with its own values for temperature, humidity, wind speed, and other factors. Its developers hope the GCRM will lead to a future generation of much more advanced and accurate climate models. Scientists also hope to use data mining, in which they extract precise locations of extreme weather events such as hurricanes from the vast amounts of climate data in global models. A third study will quantify how current human activities will affect future ocean temperatures and sea level rise. Such studies will require increasingly more powerful supercomputers.

In the future, we will look to climate scientists to predict the direction and rate of climate changes and to inform the public. But in the long run, climate scientists can only do so much. It will be up to an informed and intelligent public—both citizens and policy makers- -to make the changes that will enable future generations to adapt to climate change.

The GCRM breaks up the atmosphere into small pieces. In the full simulation, each cell is as small as 2.5 miles (4 km) across.

Timeline

1859 John Tyndall discovers heat-absorbing gases and suggests changing their concentrations could cause climate change.

1896 Svante Arrhenius publishes the first calculations relating global warming to human carbon dioxide emissions.

1897 Thomas Chamberlin develops a model for global carbon exchange.

1924 Milutin Milankovitch publishes a theory proposing that minor changes in Earth's orbit cause ice ages.

1938 Guy Stewart Callendar argues that global warming, caused by greenhouse gases released during fossil fuel combustion, is presently occurring.

1956 Gilbert N. Plass calculates that doubling carbon dioxide would cause a rise in temperature.

1957 Roger Revelle determines carbon dioxide produced by humans is not readily absorbed by the oceans.

1958 Charles Keeling begins daily measurements of atmospheric carbon dioxide levels at Mauna Loa, Hawaii. These measurements continue today.

1966 Cesare Emiliani studies oxygen isotopes in deep-sea fossils.

1970 The National Oceanic and Atmospheric Administration is created and becomes the world's leading funder of climate research.

1988 The Intergovernmental Panel on Climate Change (IPCC) is established. It produces increasingly urgent reports in 1990, 1995, 2001, 2007, and 2014.

1992 A Rio de Janeiro conference results in the UN Framework Convention on Climate Change (UNFCCC).

1997 The Kyoto Protocol, an amendment to the UNFCCC, is adopted. It sets internationally binding targets for the reduction of greenhouse gas emissions.

2005 On February 16, the Kyoto treaty goes into effect, signed by all industrial nations except the United States.

2006 Michael Mann's hockey stick graph, first published in 1998, is validated; the film *An Inconvenient Truth*, about Al Gore's attempts to educate the public about global warming, is released.

2009 In November, e-mails from the Climatic Research Unit of the University of East Anglia are stolen and published on the Internet, resulting in a scandal.

2012 The Arctic ice cap reaches a new low.

2014 Atmospheric carbon dioxide levels top 400 ppm; the fifth IPCC report is released.

Essential Facts

Computer Climate Models

During the 1960s and 1970s, climate scientists used new digital computers to develop climate models describing global processes controlling climate. New data was constantly entered into the models, improving their accuracy.

Weather Satellites

NASA and NOAA both developed satellite programs. At first the satellites were used only for weather forecasting, but they soon began collecting long-term climate data.

IMPACT ON SCIENCE

The study of climate science has led to new breakthroughs in the understanding of greenhouse gases, including ozone, CFCs, nitrogen and sulfur oxides, and methane. In the 1970s and 1980s, the importance of many of these gases to climate was discovered. Proxy data, which is widely used throughout many branches of science, has a deep connection with climate science. Proxy data from tree rings, ocean sediments, and ice cores has added to data on ancient climates and increased understanding of climate cycles.

POLITICAL IMPACT

Climate change has become a hotly debated political issue in recent decades. Politicians and a minority of scientists have suggested that climate change is not a serious issue, that it is not as severe as experts predict, or even that it does not exist at all. By 2014, overwhelming evidence had been collected showing climate change is happening and human activity has contributed significantly to it. Though the issue has been settled scientifically, it remains politically controversial.

QUOTE

"The graph told a simple story: that a sharp and highly unusual rise in atmospheric warming was occurring on Earth. Furthermore, that rise seemed to coincide with human-caused increases in greenhouse gas levels due to the burning of fossil fuels."

—*Climate scientist Michael Mann*

$$\frac{a+b}{a} = \frac{a}{b} = 1,618$$

Glossary

airborne fraction

The percentage of fossil fuel–based dioxide emissions that remain in the atmosphere.

chlorofluorocarbons (CFCs)

Human-made industrial chemicals having a potent greenhouse gas effect that also break down stratospheric ozone.

clathrate

An ice-like substance found in seabed sediments around the world that releases methane as the sediments melt.

climate

The average state of the atmosphere at a given place and time, usually measured over a period of 30 years.

climate science

The modern study of climate and the interacting processes that cause it.

climatology

The early science of describing climate, which was considered to be static and unchanging.

greenhouse effect

The process by which gases in the atmosphere absorb and re-radiate heat from Earth's surface.

greenhouse gas

A gas, such as carbon dioxide or methane, that traps heat in the atmosphere and keeps the planet warm.

hockey stick graph

A graph first released in 1999, showing that global temperatures were relatively stable for 900 of the last 1,000 years but have increased rapidly since 1900.

ice core

A long cylinder of ice obtained by drilling down through a glacier or ice sheet; used to analyze ancient climates.

infrared radiation

Heat, or long-wave radiation; light with a wavelength longer than red and shorter than microwaves.

isotope

A variant of an element that has the same number of protons but a different number of neutrons in each atom.

Keeling Curve

A plot of steadily rising atmospheric carbon dioxide concentrations from 1958 through present, based on readings from Mauna Loa, Hawaii.

meteorology

The study of weather.

methane

A hydrocarbon produced naturally in wetlands and rice paddies, now increasing due to human activities; most common greenhouse gas after water vapor and carbon dioxide.

model

A simplified representation of a system, used to study complex systems such as climate.

permafrost

Frozen soil, sometimes many meters deep, found in the tundra of the Northern Hemisphere; now melting and releasing methane due to global warming.

proxy data

Indirect measurements from ice cores, tree rings, and other sources that serve as substitutes or stand-ins for temperature measurements in studies of ancient climates.

sediment core

A long cylinder of sediment drilled from the ocean floor downward; used to determine ancient climates.

Additional Resources

Selected Bibliography

"Climate Modeling 101." *National Academy of Sciences*. US Government, 2012. Web. 21 Apr. 2014.

Weart, Spencer. "The Discovery of Global Warming." *American Institute of Physics*. American Institute of Physics, Feb. 2014. Web. 30 Apr. 2014.

Further Readings

Cherry, Lynne, and Gary Braasch. *How We Know What We Know about Our Changing Climate: Scientists and Kids Explore Global Warming*. Nevada City, CA: Dawn, 2008. Print.

Woodward, John. *Climate Change*. New York: DK, 2011. Print.

Websites

To learn more about History of Science, visit **booklinks.abdopublishing.com**. These links are routinely monitored and updated to provide the most current information available.

National Aeronautics and Space Administration (NASA)

NASA Headquarters
Suite 2R40
Washington, DC 20546
202-358-0001

http://www.nasa.gov

NASA is the US government agency responsible for space exploration and research. This includes a satellite program geared to the study of global climate change.

National Oceanic and Atmospheric Administration (NOAA)

1401 Constitution Avenue, NW
Room 5128
Washington, DC 20230
301-713-1208

http://www.noaa.gov

NOAA is a government agency that does research and education related to the oceans and atmosphere. Weather and climate, including the study of global climate change, are key aspects of its mission.

Source Notes

Chapter 1. The Hockey Stick of Climate

1. "How Much Has the Global Temperature Risen in the Last 100 Years?" *University Corporation for Atmospheric Research.* UCAR, 2014. Web. 16 May 2014.

2. "Consensus." *Global Climate Change.* NASA, n.d. Web. 12 Sept. 2014.

3. Michael E. Mann. "Interview with Michael Mann, Author of The Hockey Stick and the Climate Wars: Dispatches from the Front Lines." *Columbia* UP. Columbia University, 2012. Web. 7 May 2014.

4. "Age of the Earth." *United States Geological Survey.* USGS, 9 July 2007. Web. 9 May 2014.

5. Michael E. Mann, Raymond S. Bradley, and Malcolm K. Hughes. "Northern Hemisphere Temperatures during the Past Millennium: Inferences, Uncertainties, and Limitations." *Geophysical Research Letters* 26.6 (1999): 759–762. Print.

6. John Cook. "What Evidence Is There for the Hockey Stick?" *Skeptical Science.* Skeptical Science, 20 July 2010. Web. 9 May 2014.

7. "Earth Warmer Today Than during 70 to 80 Percent of the Past 11,300 Years." *Oregon State University.* Science Daily, 7 Mar. 2013. Web. 16 May 2014.

8. Ibid.

9. Ibid.

10. S. Fred Singer. "The Inventor of the Global Warming Hockey Stick Doubles Down." *American Thinker.* American Thinker, 21 Jan. 2014. Web. 12 Sept. 2014.

11. David Appell. "Behind the Hockey Stick." *Scientific American.* Scientific American, 21 Feb. 2005. Web. 7 May 2014.

Chapter 2. The Early Years of Climate Science

1. Spencer Weart. "The Carbon Dioxide Greenhouse Effect." *American Institute of Physics.* American Institute of Physics, Feb. 2014. Web. 12 Sept. 2014.

2. Ibid.

Chapter 3. Climate Science in the Early 1900s

1. "A Half Century of Crisis 1900–1950 CE." *World History for Us All.* San Diego State University and UCLA, n.d. Web. 12 May 2014.

2. Ibid.

3. Spencer Weart. "Climatology as a Profession." *American Institute of Physics.* American Institute of Physics, Aug. 2012. Web. 12 Sept. 2014.

4. Fraser Cain. "The Tilt of the Earth." *Universe Today.* Universe Today, 10 Mar. 2009. Web. 12 May 2014.

5. "Astronomical Theory of Climate Change." *NOAA.* NOAA, 6 Apr. 2009. Web. 12 May 2014.

6. "Seeing the Light: G.S. Callendar and Carbon Dioxide Theory of Climate Change." *University of Manchester.* University of Manchester, 2010. Web. 12 May 2014.

7. "The Atmosphere of Venus." *HyperPhysics.* Georgia State University, n.d. Web. 15 May 2014.

8. Ibid.

9. Tim Sharp. "Earth's Atmosphere: Composition, Climate, & Weather." *Space.com.* Purch, 19 Sept. 2012. Web. 12 Sept. 2014.

Chapter 4. Climate Science Heats Up

1. Spencer Weart. "The Carbon Dioxide Greenhouse Effect." *American Institute of Physics.* American Institute of Physics, Feb. 2014. Web. 12 Sept. 2014.

2. Ibid.

3. Ibid.

4. R. F. Keeling, S. C. Piper, A. F. Bollenbacher, and J. S. Walker. "Atmospheric Carbon Dioxide Record from Mauna Loa." *Carbon Dioxide Information Analysis Center*. CDIAC, 26 Sept. 2012. Web. 12 Sept. 2014.

5. Marshall Brain. "How Carbon-14 Dating Works." *How Stuff Works*. How Stuff Works, 2014. Web. 12 Sept. 2014.

6. "Keeling Curve." *Climate Central*. Climate Central, 1 May 2013. Web. 17 Apr. 2014.

7. Chris Jones, Peter Cox, and Chris Huntingford. "The Atmospheric CO2 Airborne Fraction and Carbon Cycle Feedbacks." *Met Office Hadley Centre*. Met Office Hadley Centre, 2007. Web. 16 June 2014.

Chapter 5. The Rise of Atmospheric Science

1. Spencer Weart. "The Carbon Dioxide Greenhouse Effect." *American Institute of Physics*. American Institute of Physics, Feb. 2014. Web. 12 Sept. 2014.

2. Ibid.

3. "Frequently Asked Questions." *Scripps CO2 Program*. Scripps Institution of Oceanography, 2014. Web. 19 May 2014.

4. Kiley Kroh. "Carbon Dioxide Levels Just Hit Their Highest Point in 800,000 Years." *Climate Progress*. Climate Progress, 30 Apr. 2014. Web. 12 Sept. 2014.

5. Richard B. Alley. *The Two-Mile Time Machine: Ice Cores, Abrupt Climate Change, and Our Future*. Princeton, NJ: Princeton UP, 2000. Print. 12–13, 25.

6. "The GISP2 Ice Coring Effort." *National Climatic Data Center*. NOAA, 1995. Web. 21 May 2014.

7. Spencer Weart. "Other Greenhouse Gases." *American Institute of Physics*. American Institute of Physics, Feb. 2014. Web. 12 Sept. 2014.

8. Ibid.

9. Ibid.

10. Ibid.

11. "Methane Emissions." *Overview of Greenhouse Gases*. EPA, 17 Apr. 2014. Web. 21 May 2014.

12. Ibid.

Chapter 6. Evidence for Warming Builds

1. Spencer Weart. "The Discovery of Global Warming." *American Institute of Physics*. American Institute of Physics, May 2010. Web. 12 Sept. 2014.

2. Spencer Weart. "The Public and Climate Change." *American Institute of Physics*. American Institute of Physics, Feb. 2014. Web. 12 Sept. 2014.

3. Ibid.

4. Spencer Weart. "International Cooperation." *American Institute of Physics*. American Institute of Physics, Feb. 2014. Web. 12 Sept. 2014.

5. "20th Century Drought." *National Climatic Data Center*. NOAA, n.d. Web. 21 May 2014.

6. Spencer Weart. "Rapid Climate Change." *American Institute of Physics*. American Institute of Physics, Feb. 2014. Web. 12 Sept. 2014.

Source Notes Continued

7. "Climate of 1998 Annual Review." *National Climatic Data Center*. NOAA, 12 Jan. 1999. Web. 28 May 2014.

8. Ibid.

9. Ibid.

10. James Wright. "What Do the 'Climategate' Hacked CRU Emails Tell Us?" *Skeptical Science*. Skeptical Science, 15 Jan. 2011. Web. 12 Sept. 2014.

11. Leo Hickman. "Police Close Investigation into Hacked Climate Science Emails." *Guardian*. Guardian, 18 July 2012. Web. 3 May 2014.

12. "United Nations Framework Convention on Climate Change (UNFCCC)." *World Meteorological Organization*. United Nations, n.d. Web. 23 May 2014.

13. Peter Saundry. "Kyoto Protocol and the United States." *Encyclopedia of Earth*. Encyclopedia of Earth, 26 Feb. 2013. Web. 12 Sept. 2014.

14. "Who's On Board with the Copenhagen Accord?" *US Climate Action Network*. US Climate Action Network, 2014. Web. 23 May 2014.

15. Bob Lacatena. "Is Al Gore's 'An Inconvenient Truth' Accurate?" *Skeptical Science*. Skeptical Science, 7 Jan. 2014. Web 22 May 2014.

Chapter 7. The Rise of Climate Modeling

1. Gavin Schmidt. "Wrong but Useful." *Physics World*. Physics World, 1 Oct. 2009. Web. 22 May 2014.

2. "Tapping the Earth Simulator." *University of Colorado*. University Corporation for Atmospheric Research, Apr. 2004. Web. 16 June 2014.

3. Ibid.

4. Serkan Toto. "NEC Updates Its Supercomputer 'Earth Simulator System,' Breaks Record." *Tech Crunch*. Tech Crunch, 4 June 2009. Web. 16 June 2014.

5. Adam Scaife, Chris Folland, and John Mitchell. "A Model Approach to Climate Change." *Physics World*. Physics World, 1 Feb. 2007. Web. 22 May 2014.

6. Michael E. Mann. "Earth Will Cross the Climate Danger Threshold by 2036." *Scientific American*. Scientific American, 18 Mar. 2014. Web. 10 May 2014.

Chapter 8. Climate Change Today

1. Michael E. Mann. "How Do We Know Humans Are Responsible for Global Warming?" *Weather Underground*. Weather Underground, n.d. Web. 22 Apr. 2014.

2. Seth Borenstein. "Arctic Ice Shrinks to All-Time Low; Half 1980 Size." *Associated Press*. Associated Press, 19 Sept. 2012. Web. 26 May 2014.

3. Ibid.

4. Ibid.

5. "Why Did Earth's Surface Temperature Stop Rising in the Past Decade?" *Climate.gov*. NOAA, 8 Nov. 2013. Web. 27 May 2014.

6. "Global Analysis—Annual 2012." *National Climatic Data Center*. NOAA, Jan. 2013. Web. 10 May 2014.

7. Gina-Marie Cheeseman. "EPA Data Shows US Greenhouse Gas Emissions Slightly Decreased in 2012." *TriplePundit*. TriplePundit, 18 Apr. 2014. Web. 20 Apr. 2014.

8. Thomas M. Kostigen. "Government Lists 2013's Most Extreme Weather Events: 6 Takeaways." *National Geographic*. National Geographic, 22 Jan. 2014. Web. 26 May 2014.

9. "NASA Scientists React to 400 ppm Carbon Milestone." *Global Climate Change*. NASA, n.d. Web. 28 May 2014.

Chapter 9. Climate Change Tomorrow

1. "Climate Change 'Has Moved Firmly into the Present,' US Report Says." *Associated Press*. Associated Press, 6 May 2014. Web. 12 Sept. 2014.

2. Valerie Volcovici. "White House Unveils Dire Warning, Calls for Action on Climate." *Reuters*. Reuters, 6 May 2014. Web. 12 Sept. 2014.

3. Brian Clark Howard. "Federal Climate Change Report Highlights Risks for Americans." *National Geographic Daily News*. National Geographic, 6 May 2014. Web. 15 May 2014.

4. Seth Borenstein. "Final Fed Climate Report Will Present Dire Picture." *Associated Press*. Associated Press, 6 May 2014. Web. 6 May 2014.

5. Lindsay Abrams. "IPCC Report: The Top 10 Ways to Avert a Climate Catastrophe." *Salon.com*. Salon.com, Apr. 2014. Web. 16 Apr. 2014.

6. Michael E. Mann. "Earth Will Cross the Climate Danger Threshold by 2036." *Scientific American*. Scientific American, 18 Mar. 2014. Web. 10 May 2014.

7. Andrea Thompson. "Storm Surge Could Flood NYC 1 in Every 4 Years." *Climate Central*. Climate Central, 25 Apr. 2014. Web. 19 May 2014.

8. Joe Romm. "Conservative Climate Panel Warns World Faces 'Breakdown of Food Systems' and More Violent Conflict." *Climate Progress*. Climate Progress, 30 Mar. 2014. Web. 31 Mar. 2014.

9. Ibid.

10. Phil Plait. "West Antarctic Glacier Slow-Speed Collapse May Be Unstoppable." *Bad Astronomy*. Slate, 12 May 2014. Web. 13 May 2014.

11. "Sea Level Rise." *The Ocean*. National Geographic, 2014. Web. 12 Sept. 2014.

12. Ibid.

13. Bill McKibben. "Global Warming's Terrifying New Math." *Rolling Stone*. Rolling Stone, 19 July 2012. Web. 29 Jan. 2014.

Index

About the Author

Carol Hand has a PhD in zoology with a specialization in marine ecology and a special interest in environmental and climate science. Before becoming a science writer, she taught college, wrote for standardized testing companies, and developed multimedia science curricula. She has written more than 20 books for young people on topics including glaciers, environmental engineering, and biomass energy.